# DAVID ST. CLAIR'S LESSONS IN INSTANT ESP

# DAVID ST. CLAIR'S LESSONS IN INSTANT ESP

by
David St. Clair

PRENTICE-HALL, INC., Englewood Cliffs, N.J.

For Lexie Kinsler of California
Patt Cobb of Mexico
Carole Hedin of Canada
Eric Reishaaver of South Africa
. . . whose lives have been profoundly changed by this
course.

*David St. Clair's Lessons in Instant ESP*
by David St. Clair
Copyright © 1978 by David St. Clair
Printed in the United States of America
Prentice-Hall International, Inc., London
Prentice-Hall of Australia, Pty. Ltd., Sydney
Prentice-Hall of Canada, Ltd., Toronto
Prentice-Hall of India Private Ltd., New Delhi
Prentice-Hall of Japan, Inc., Tokyo
Prentice-Hall of Southeast Asia Pte. Ltd., Singapore
Whitehall Books Limited, Wellington, New Zealand
10  9  8  7  6

Library of Congress Cataloging in Publication Data
St. Clair, David.
        David St. Clair's Lessons in instant ESP.
        Includes index.
        1. Extrasensory perception.    I. Title.    II. Title:
Lessons in instant ESP.
BF1321.S25        133.8        77-17152
ISBN 0-13-197137-9

# Contents

# An Introduction to the Psychic Development Class That Really Works

The first question you're going to ask is: "With all the ESP books on the market today, why *another* book?"

The answer is that most of the other ESP books *don't work* for their readers. This book will. I have taught these ideas and these techniques all across the United States and as far away as South Africa.

And they work.

The entire psychic and occult field has been going through a lot of changes lately. During the 1960s and part of the 1970s it was in full swing. Everyone talked about ESP and devoured all the books on it they could find. So many books came out that the devourers got a stomachache and started eating in select choice bites. Many people, pleased to learn that ESP and psychic healing really worked, said, "Oh, isn't that nice," and went on to other fields of interest.

Still others, more personally aroused, looked in vain for methods on how they could incorporate this realm of knowledge into their everyday lives. There were a few how-to books quickly churned out and an awful lot of fly-by-night teachers. The problem was that most of the books and teachers dwelled on pseudo-spiritual things rather than try to make psychic matters practical. Those who were searching for a personal message in it, soon found their interest waning. The vast majority of readers got caught up in the new wave of occult books like *The Exorcist, The Omen, The Bermuda Triangle,* and *I Was Caught in the Devil's Armpit* kind of thing and wouldn't read any psychic book unless it scared them half silly. Half silly is where they have remained, and the entire field has come around to ghost stories and things that go bump in the night. So today you will meet people who truly believe in the

1

psychic field but who have purposely tuned themselves out of it. Instead of being considered avant-garde, as someone with an interest in the psychic would have been in the late 1950s, today you might find your interest in the psychic being disclaimed as "old-fashioned." *Sic transit* American fashions.

When I was growing up (and I won't tell you how many years ago that was, so don't ask!) I never heard psychic things referred to except in the form of ghost stories. At Halloween we never understood what witches were really all about. Psychic readers were always gypsies who asked you to cross one palm with silver while the other palm was lifting your wallet, and a medium was something between small and large.

I got hooked on the whole business early when, at the age of about six or seven, I heard the voice of my dead great-aunt talking to my grandmother. I heard my grandmother reply (until she fainted, when she realized that her sister had been dead for several years), and I heard the answers that the "ghost" gave. Of course, one didn't discuss things like this in polite company, and so I became a sort of "closet investigator" as I searched the library in Warren, Ohio, for books on what I'd seen and heard.

Naturally, there were none. The librarian expected me (and everyone else in town) to be content with the Bobbsey Twins and Dickens. But every now and then in some tattered copy of *Amazing Tales* or *Supernatural Stories* I read of "lost books of knowledge," "alchemists' secrets," or "forgotten lore" that I could never get my hands on in Ohio.

When I was seventeen I sent away for the Rosicrucians' mail-order lessons and followed their instructions diligently until one night I found myself out of my body. This hadn't even been hinted at in the lesson and it scared the hell out of me. I didn't know such a thing was possible, and when I wrote to the Rosicrucians to tell of the awesome experience, they wrote back that it was "very interesting." I had expected a better answer (and to this day I believe I deserved one), and so I promptly canceled the rest of the course. (In this book, you too will learn to leave your body. However, you will understand *what* you are doing and *how* you are doing it.)

As I grew older and kept on the lookout for strange phenomena and coincidences, more and more of them happened to me. Not that I was anyone special. It's just that when you set your mind to something, more of that "something" will appear to it. That is a fact that we will explore later on in the course.

Anyway, psychic things kept happening to me and I got to the point when I *knew* that certain things would happen to other people, I knew when someone was going to call me on the phone; when someone was writing me a letter. I knew when I would meet a friend as I turned a street corner. I knew what was in a package before I opened it. I knew when someone was lying to me. I knew when someone was going to die. When I went to South America and worked for *Time* and *Life* magazines I had the opportunity to observe many psychic events and began to include them in my normal news stories. Naturally, *Time* magazine threw most of these references out of the final edited copy, but I started looking for inexplicable happenings to explain things that seemingly had no meaning. This searching eventually became a book, and when I returned to the United States I did more research and wrote more books. Then I began to share what I had learned with others and thus the teaching part of it came about. I am now a member of the American Society for Psychical Research, The Brazilian Society for Psychical Research, and Psychic Research Society of London, and am a recent past president of the California Society for Psychical Research.

Among my books on the subject are *Drum & Candle; The Psychic World of California; Psychic Healers; How Your Psychic Powers Can Make You Rich; Pagans, Priests, and Prophets;* and *Watseka*, a strange true story I put into fiction form.

In November of 1975 I was invited to go to Johannesburg, South Africa, where Reeva Beauty Products was sponsoring a class on how to use psychic techniques in business. The owner of the firm, Ms. Reeva Foreman, herself a graduate of Mind Dynamics and a disciple of the late William Penn Patrick and his "Holiday Magic" cosmetic pyramid-empire, knew the value of psychic training for her salespeople. She herself had applied it with "Holiday Magic" to make as much as $100,000 a month in sales. But she had discovered that, like TM and est, Mind Dynamics gave a brief high and then faded soon after.

She brought a parapsychologist and a psychic to South Africa and asked me to come along because she had read several of my books, liked them, and wanted to present an "author" to the students and to the uptight South African press.

I sat through a Thursday night, Friday night, and all day Saturday of astrology, and why numerology can help you find a mate, and the secret symbols on the tarot cards. I realized that while this was very interesting, the students were not learning how to apply anything to their business activities. After all, the reason they had paid their $175 for this course was to become better salespeople.

So I asked the parapsychologist if I could teach class on Sunday. He, wanting to visit a gold mine that was open to visitors on Sundays only, readily agreed.

I took over the class at 9 that morning and carried it through till 6 that night. During the session I taught the students how to know—by touch—if a document (contract, letter, or such) was truthful or not; showed them how to convince a client that he needed a product just by sitting across the desk from him; and demonstrated how they could set up a positive vibration for their sales pitch *before* they met face to face with their client. I showed them how to turn negativity into positiveness right at the client's door. I showed them how to use their inner abilities to get anything they *really* wanted. Every one of the students told Ms. Foreman that my one day was worth the entire course. Six months later I learned that sales had *more than doubled* when her sales people began using my techniques.

On my return to Los Angeles, I worked up a four-day course (Thursday night, Friday night, Saturday, and Sunday) in which people were taught to go within, to tap their full potential, to bring this potential to the surface, and *to direct it* toward what they wanted.

The results were startling not only to my students, but to me as well, for in all the classes that I have given (in California, Arizona, Texas, Oregon, Ohio, Canada, Mexico, and England) *there has not been one person* who was unable to do these things! And these "things" ranged from ESP with a complete stranger to leaving their bodies, going to a definite location, and returning. Having seen positive results in groups of complete strangers, I *know* these methods work.

Why fool around with this psychic nonsense? Why get mixed up in kooky things? Why sit around with a bunch of crazies and "feel" the aura, "communicate" with the dead, "leave" your body? Why worry about your "hidden" abilities (whatever that may mean) when it's all you can do to cope with your "obvious" abilities?

Why indeed?

Well, let me rephrase the above.

Why read the classics when you can just as well spend your time with paperback potboilers?

Why go to the theater when you can stay home and watch T.V.?

Why eat a sirloin steak when a Big Mac is just as filling?

Why take photos in color when the image is just as clear in black and white?

You get the idea? Sure, you can plod along day by day in the same old rut! Why not! Millions of your fellow lemmings are doing exactly that. Sure, you can stay in the same unfulfilling job, live in the same drab house, and spend your time with your same dull friends. Why not? After all, twenty-four hours of boredom and nonattainment is the same thing as twenty-four hours of excitement and accomplishment. Right?

Why do anything that will increase your enjoyment of life? Why bother to better yourself; to raise your abilities to a level where you will win not only newfound respect from your friends and co-workers but newfound respect for yourself *from* yourself?

You are *you*. *You are unique.* Even in a crowded, impersonal city *there is no other person exactly like you.* Sure, they've got fingers and toes and one head and two kneecaps, but they don't have what goes on in *your* head. They don't have *your* dreams and *your* plans and *your* particular talents. *You* have them, and in a unique combination that creates a unique *you*. A fascinating you. An exceptional you.

More people are realizing this every day, and so there is an increasing search for ideas that will help individuals realize their true potential. Methods and techniques that can be done at home either alone or with a few friends are in demand. The average American has come to understand that he is more than flesh and blood and is capable of more than just acquiring

5

material things. The techniques in this book will enable you, the average reader, to develop your own innate abilities—call them psychic abilities if you choose—to live a life more fulfilling in every way, and even get the material things you desire. This book will also give a lot of people the ego boost of telling their friends: "Hey, look what I can do!"

I've tried to put into this book everything I've learned in over twenty-five years of study of these psychic techniques. But, even though I use the word "technique," the book isn't "technical." It is light and breezy and humorous because I've found that people pay attention when they are enjoying themselves. If they start laughing, they will pay attention: they don't want to miss the next punch line. No matter how sincere they are in wanting to develop their inner abilities, people won't sit through two nights and two days of boredom. My classes aren't boring, and I don't intend to make this book boring. It contains the complete course—Thursday and Friday nights, all day Saturday and Sunday—and explains, as I personally explain to my students, how to use your psychic resources to the fullest. Case histories, using actual names of students from my classes who have done all the things described, are included.

This book also includes the following:

(1) *The three levels of the mind–Conscious, Sub-Conscious* and *Super-Conscious.* What they are, where they are, and how each level can be contacted to solve different problems. (For instance, there is a surefire method to remember any name or fact you've ever really learned at any time in your life. I've had people go back as far as fifty-five years and recall a name from their school days.)

(2) *The Little Man in your Sub-Conscious mind.* How he works, what he can do if prodded, and his ability to contact the Super-Conscious to give you *any* information you desire. This is where all creativity and ideas spring from.

(3) *How the mind affects the physical body.* How to make any part of your body feel the effects of the Sub-Conscious mind. This, of course, leads into techniques for self-healing and general good health: how to get rid of a headache or a pain in the back, and why some cancer specialists are using psychic methods to help terminally ill patients. This goes much further than "the power of positive thinking" ever thought of going.

(4) *Reaching the Cosmic Forces.* What they are, where they originate, and how they can be tapped to do anything a person wishes by means of a never-fail method that includes healing, information gathering, and ESP contacting. I consider this one of the most important things I have ever learned in this lifetime. I use it constantly. It works.

(5) *Overcoming insomnia.* How to fall asleep every night. It's worked with people who have been on pills for years. My students no longer need sleeping pills. Neither do I.

(6) *Your "secret place."* How to get there, what to do when you are there, and how to come back to "the surface" feeling refreshed and energized. The technique you will learn uses a color progression and is better than TM because it's not a boring mantra. It's as good as eight hours' sleep.

(7) *Contacting anyone anywhere in the world.* Sounds like a big order, but it's quite simple once you know the basics.

(8) *Making an impression on a businessman before you even get into his office.* Convincing him to listen to you, to buy your product (whether it be a vacuum cleaner or your own talents) before you sit down across from him. What to do while you are there to make certain you get what you want from him. This has been especially beneficial for people looking for a job, trying to make a sale, or getting in to see an executive who is always "in conference."

(9) *True ESP.* How students who have just met make contact and begin to read each other's minds. We start with something easy like a color and quickly graduate to names and numbers. This ability is then tested when the individuals are separated by walls or freeway miles.

(10) *Psychometry.* What it is and how you know when you are doing it. How to *not-interpret* what you get. How to relax and receive impressions without going into trance. Then, how to use this knowledge to see what's in a sealed envelope; to "see" if a contract should be signed or not; to "feel" whether a person is telling the truth; and to "read" someone's personality in the instant of a handshake.

(11) *Seeing the aura.* What it is, what the colors signify, and how to interpret them when you are trying to make a sale or convince someone to go along with you. How to see your own aura as well.

(12) *Healing.* All aspects, including healing in person as well as at a distance. What the energies are, where they come from, and why they are not limited by time or space. Healing of small children and animals. Healing someone who doesn't want to be healed. Healing the mentally ill. The power behind a healing circle.

(13) *The Pentagram.* Where it came from and how we can use it in today's world. An almost surefire method of obtaining any *material* object you desire.

(14) *Automatic writing.* How to know if that's really a "spirit" pushing the pencil in your hand or whether it's all in *your* mind. How to use it and not let it use you.

(15) *Regression into a past life.* How to do it. How not to do it. The dangers involved but the satisfaction gained if it is handled correctly. I do this just once in each class, but the effect is stunning—even in jaded Hollywood!

(16) *Seeing others' past lives.* I've developed a method in which students pair off and each is able to see other faces appearing across his or her partner's features. It's really amazing when they get started, and almost always these past lives have a special significance for the individual in the present.

(17) *Astral travel.* In this lesson students learn how to leave their bodies and travel elsewhere in time and space. For instance, I get the students to relax and then leave their bodies to visit a friend. Then, at the lunch break, they call the person visited to verify their experience of what he or she was doing, wearing, and so on at the time of the visit. The rate of accuracy is always amazing—and more often than not the friend has admitted to have been *thinking* of the psychic visitor at the very moment of the visit.

(18) I also plan to bring in, just for the fun of it, some other techniques not covered in the usual ESP book—*table tipping,* for example. The old-fashioned way to get the energies aroused and then—look out: The table will seem to move with its own physical and mental powers. I have taught classes during which a card table has actually raised up on two legs and chased me around the room, with the students trying to keep their hands on its top. Once, one continued for about ten feet across a thick carpet after the students took their hands away.

(19) *An old-fashioned séance.* The works: the candles, the incense, the music, the deck of cards. How to hold one and

what to do when things start happening. (Once a small kitten materialized under the open palm of a student who was in a semitrance. Almost everyone at the table saw the animal, and all who did agreed on its size, coloration, and the exact time it vanished.)

As far as I know—and I've done a great deal of research into this—there is no other course teaching psychic development and how to apply it in everyday situations. My aim is not to create a bunch of mediums or a gaggle of palm readers. I am interested in the practicality—not the kookiness—of these energies. And, as far as I know, there is no book on the market today that teaches a reader not only *how* to tap his psychic sources and *how* to use them, but (and this is so important) *why* these energies work and *why* they obey commands.

Which brings us back to my first question: Why try to develop your psychic powers? Because life is too damned short to go through it with blinders on. Because the world is a fantastic place and becomes even more so when you know all its secrets and can use them at will. Because you care about yourself enough to better yourself. And you can be better. (If you're satisfied with yourself as you are now, my congratulations!) You can be even better than your dreams.

Now at this point, you may be saying to yourself, "Stop all this bull. I've heard it all before, and I've read it all before, and I'm still the same person I always have been." If so, then you should do one of two things:

1) Close this book and go back to being your satisfied self.

2) As you keep this book open and read further, keep your *mind* open as well. Soak up what I have to say without prejudice and without criticism. Store it away in your Sub-Conscious, and when it has been digested—and *only* then—make your decision.

I don't ask you to believe anything I have to say. All I ask is that you receive it with an open mind, and then judge. Fair enough?

Want to continue? Fine. Let's get down to basics.

# LESSON 1
# Energy

Knowing all these things I'm going to teach you doesn't make me Emperor of the World or give me the ego stimulus of setting myself up as a professional medium. I don't feel I am "touched by God" or "in communication with my spirit guides" or "ordained into the secret brotherhood." I understand that I know these things because I took the trouble to stop and listen.

*To stop and listen to myself.* (Too bad this isn't a multicolored book, because I'd like that last sentence printed in red.)

I learned to stop and listen to myself, and *to pay attention to what I heard,* and then, in most cases, *to act upon what I had heard.* (More red ink, please.)

Listen . . .

Pay attention . . .

Act.

That's the A.B.C. (or the L.P.A.) behind all psychic ability.

If you don't *listen,* you won't hear the information as it is given to you. If you don't *pay attention* to the information and evaluate it, then the information won't be doing you any good. If you don't *act* upon that information once you've figured out how to use it, then it might as well have been shouted into the wind or flushed down the toilet for all the good it was to you.

Listen. Pay attention. Act.

Before we go any further and get into the power that your mind actually has, I want you to take a test—a simple test whose results are of interest to no one but you. Don't try and guess the answers that *I* would like. They're not for me, but for yourself, to tell you where you are now and where you need to direct your studies for improvement in certain areas. If your reply to a question is "No," circle numeral 1. If your reply is "Sometimes," circle numeral 2. If your reply is a definite "Yes," circle numeral 3.

Remember: Answer the questions truthfully. Give them some thought.

## TENSION

|  | No | Sometimes | Yes |
|---|---|---|---|
| 1. I experience feelings of tension. | 1 | 2 | 3 |
| 2. I am more critical than is necessary. | 1 | 2 | 3 |
| 3. I experience feelings of insecurity. | 1 | 2 | 3 |

| | No | Sometimes | Yes |
|---|---|---|---|
| 4. I have poor emotional control. | 1 | 2 | 3 |
| 5. I have difficulty coping with situations I cannot control. | 1 | 2 | 3 |
| 6. I am a perfectionist. | 1 | 2 | 3 |
| 7. I consider myself nervous and high-strung. | 1 | 2 | 3 |
| 8. People tell me I am too "uptight." | 1 | 2 | 3 |
| 9. My feelings of tension increase in certain situations. | 1 | 2 | 3 |
| 10. I worry more than is necessary. | 1 | 2 | 3 |

Now add up the numerals you have circled and put the total here:     TOTAL _____

## ANXIETY

| | No | Sometimes | Yes |
|---|---|---|---|
| 1. I get unnecessarily concerned about relatively minor things. | 1 | 2 | 3 |
| 2. I do not understand why I have certain fears. | 1 | 2 | 3 |
| 3. Some of my fears are not rational. | 1 | 2 | 3 |
| 4. I have difficulty trusting people. | 1 | 2 | 3 |
| 5. I re-do things to make sure I've done them correctly. | 1 | 2 | 3 |
| 6. I am a failure. | 1 | 2 | 3 |
| 7. There are a few things I know I do well. | 1 | 2 | 3 |
| 8. I overanalyze everything. | 1 | 2 | 3 |
| 9. I am quite insecure. | 1 | 2 | 3 |
| 10. It takes me forever to make a decision. | 1 | 2 | 3 |
| TOTAL _____ | | | |

## SELF-CONFIDENCE

| | No | Sometimes | Yes |
|---|---|---|---|
| 1. I am uncomfortable with people. | 1 | 2 | 3 |
| 2. Most people are better than I am. | 1 | 2 | 3 |
| 3. Rarely do I do anything right. | 1 | 2 | 3 |
| 4. I am introverted. | 1 | 2 | 3 |
| 5. I don't like people as a rule. | 1 | 2 | 3 |
| 6. I don't like myself. | 1 | 2 | 3 |
| 7. I am different from most other people. | 1 | 2 | 3 |
| 8. I don't complete the projects I begin. | 1 | 2 | 3 |
| 9. I think about my past failures. | 1 | 2 | 3 |
| 10. I would like to be anybody else but myself. | 1 | 2 | 3 |
| TOTAL _____ | | | |

ENERGY

And the last category, even if you don't think it belongs here:

## INSOMNIA

| | No | Sometimes | Yes |
|---|---|---|---|
| 1. I have difficulties falling asleep. | 1 | 2 | 3 |
| 2. I sleep a little bit and then wake up. | 1 | 2 | 3 |
| 3. I take pills to get to sleep. | 1 | 2 | 3 |
| 4. I have nightmares. | 1 | 2 | 3 |
| 5. My problems are on my mind when I retire. | 1 | 2 | 3 |
| 6. Any little noise wakes me up. | 1 | 2 | 3 |
| 7. I associate sleep with death. | 1 | 2 | 3 |
| 8. My sleeping habits are poor. | 1 | 2 | 3 |
| 9. I have to make a mental effort to fall asleep. | 1 | 2 | 3 |
| 10. I am afraid that if I fall asleep I will never wake up. | 1 | 2 | 3 |

TOTAL _____

Let's look at your scores.

If your total score in any one section is between 10 and 15, you don't need to worry about that particular aspect of your psyche. You've got it well under control and can afford to concentrate on other things.

If you totaled 16 to 20, you should do a small amount of work in that area, but mostly to polish it and take away some of the rough edges.

If your score was 21 to 25 for any section, then you need to work on that aspect of yourself. Keep this area in mind as we progress into the class and see how the new techniques you'll be learning can be applied to it.

If you scored 26 to 30 on any area, get started right away to work on that part of yourself. Concentrate on it and keep your eyes and ears open to any idea that can be used to help you. Don't delay. The longer you wait, the harder you'll have to work later.

Now that you've made a start at figuring out *who* you are, let's get on to *what* you are.

You are a flesh and blood radio, capable of tuning in to the special wavelengths aimed at you, able to "plug" yourself in and "tune" yourself to the frequency that's best for you and you can capture those mystical wavelengths just as radio and television sets do. And often do it better. And once you've refined your capturing process, you can become a transmitter and send your own messages to anyone you choose, anywhere in the world. Time and space mean nothing to your sending and receiving powers—but more on that later. You are a unique animal, a unique sending and receiving set.

Doubt it? Okay, let's see.

*Figure 1.*

In Figure 1, I have drawn the profile of a woman. (Please remember I'm a writer, not an artist!) There you see her with her hair neatly combed, her blouse demurely ruffled up to her neck, and her lipstick evenly (if rather heavily) in place. We could give her a name, even make up a lifetime for her, but for all that we might invent for her, *she remains nothing more than a line drawing on paper.*

Something is missing. Something vital.

Ah, hah! you say. The problem is that she is only one-dimensional. She needs to be rounded and not just flat. Okay, suppose I could make her appear off this page and give her

15

three dimensions, make a sculpture of her. Then what? She would still remain just a series of lines and angles.

Even if I could create her for you out of flesh and blood, give her muscles and bones, real hair and blood vessels, a stomach, some fingers and toes and even a heart, she would not be *alive*. She would be dead. She would be as dead as the meat you see in the butcher shop, as dead as the corpse in the funeral parlor, as dead as Venus de Milo in marble.

Why? What's missing? What does she lack? Energy. Power. She lacks *life*. Just four letters—L, I, F, E—yet not to have it means to be dead. It means not to be aware. It means, quite simply, not to *be*.

No matter how dogmatic a skeptic you are, you have to admit there is something unseen, but real, that we call energy. There's the energy that lights up the bulbs when you turn the switch on the wall. There's the energy that makes a voice come out of your radio. There's the energy that brings forth a picture from your television set.

There are unseen waves of energy all around us all the time. Where they have come from and where they're going few of us know. How many different waves there are around us nobody knows either. Science has discovered a few of them in recent years, but how many others are out there—or *in* here—no one can say. They've been around as long as the world has been around.

For example, the room you are sitting in now is filled with all kinds of energy waves and currents. Take a radio and plug it in. Now tune it in. What do you get? Noise, voices, music, commercials, and so forth, all coming from places outside into your room on radio waves. Now get yourself a television set and plug it into the wall. Same room, same electricity—and yet, the T.V. set will pick up a completely different energy field that gives you sound and a picture. Two different machines giving you two different effects, yet operating separately in the *same* room!

For those scoffers who say it's the electricity that brings in the effects, make your radio and television sets battery-operated ones. All the electricity or battery does is activate the mechanism so it can pick up those energy wavelengths that are *constantly* running through your room. You can't taste them, can't see them, can't feel them—yet they are there.

Scientists admit that they don't know a great deal about energy. They know *that* it is, of course, but they don't know *what* it is. It's amazing that in an era when we can produce electricity at will for almost all our needs, we still really don't know what it is or why it works. It *does* work, and that is enough for most of us. (I still don't understand what keeps an airplane in the air. People have tried to explain about wind currents and all that, but I don't want to believe them. I refuse to get into something that heavy that's supported only by air. The propeller must pull it along somehow, and if not, don't tell me.)

There is also an energy that flows through us. I call this *intelligent* energy, because it takes the form of thought, perception, and is just as real—and in fact may be the same—as the energy that makes the sixty-watt bulb glow in the dark or the radio blast out with the Alka-Seltzer commercial.

Everything in the psychic realm can be boiled down to energy—energy inside you, energy around you, energy coming toward you from a great distance. You'll hear a lot about energy in this course. You may even get bored with the word and wish that I would start referring to "spirits" or "guides." But I prefer "energy" because it doesn't turn off the majority of people.

Where do we get the energy we call life? How does it come to us? Don't expect the answer to that in this class, because philosophers, scientists, and priests have been trying to figure that one out for centuries. I wouldn't presume to tell you where life comes from. But I believe that life, *the life-force,* does come *into* the human body. It does come *from* somewhere, and when it comes, it sets this dead piece of meat into action. It makes things function: heart, lungs, stomach, hair, intestines, eyesight, everything. It is the powerhouse of the human body, the Consolidated Edison of the universe.

However, in order to come in and start things working, this energy has to power a certain part of the human machine. It has to power the *brain*. Without her brain, our lovely lady would not function no matter how much life-force was being pumped into her.

The brain is not the most attractive part of the body. It's grayish and blood-flecked and slimy to the touch. (But calves brains can be delicious when fried or marinated!) Nevertheless, it's into the brain that the life-force energy comes and makes everything else work. It throws the switch and turns on the brain machine, and everything inside your body begins to bleep and whistle and gurgle and groan. The brain, that messy guckey mass up there in your head, then sends the energy to the very extremities of your body, sends it and keeps it flowing in the right amount of bursts and kilowatts. Thereupon, you are *alive*.

All very well and good, you say. So what else is new? Okay. We assume that everyone has a brain (well, I've met a few who . . .). And while it's nice to know it's doing its best up there, what does all that receiving and transmitting of energy have to do with developing psychic abilities? Good question.

Your brain receives not only body energies but *mind energies* as well. (Those of you who think you get an idea in your elbow can go to the back of the room.) Your brain gets the *mind powers*. Your brain transmits those *mind powers* to you. Your brain stores those *mind powers* until you need them. Your brain is the most incredible machine on earth.

Which leads us to Lesson 2 . . .

# LESSON 2

# The "Little Man" in Your Sub-Conscious Mind

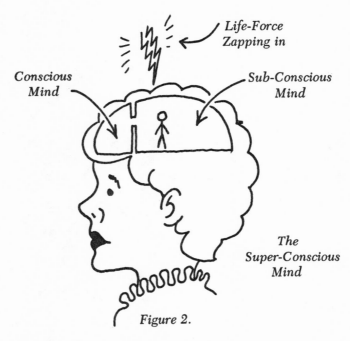

*Figure 2.*

Here you see our lady friend, in Figure 2, with a Captain Marvel lightning bolt zapping down into her brain to activate it. As you see, her brain is divided into two parts: the Conscious, up front, and the Sub-Conscious, in the back. (Now, of course these parts aren't located *exactly* this way in real life, but for our purposes, this simple diagram will serve well enough.)

Before I go any further, let me tell you that while your brain is in your head, your mind is *not*. Your mind is an outside force that comes in and powers the machine that is known as your brain. So when someone asks you where your mind is, don't point to your head. Point to just a few feet above and beyond it. The Conscious Mind is the mind that decided to buy this book. It's the mind that is presently looking at the words that have been printed here, and is the mind that is taking this information and storing it and putting it back into the Sub-Conscious part. Your Conscious Mind is also the mind that decided what shirt or blouse you were going to put on today, if you were going to take the bus or your car to work, if you were going to call your friend or not. Those are the kinds of decisions that are made on a *conscious* level—thus, by the Conscious Mind.

This part of the mind is very much at your command. Many times, in fact, *it* commands *you.* But all it does is act as a sounding board for the things you wish to do *right now,* the things you wish consciously to do. The Conscious Mind works in the here and now.

The Sub-Conscious is a really interesting part of your mind. Situated in the "back," it has two very important functions. The first one is going on all the time and you are really not aware of it. This is the Sub-Conscious Mind's supervisory aspect, which keeps you going. It makes sure that your body functions are working, makes your hair grow, makes your heart beat, makes your blood flow, digests your food, eliminates the waste matter, and so on.

Normally, you do not have to worry about any of this, since such things are taken care of automatically by that Little Man that you see standing back there in Figure 2. This Little Man is there to make sure that the *mechanical* you is functioning correctly at all times. (A little later we'll get into what he can do when dysfunction sets in.) The nice part of him is that he saves you so much worry, since he's taken care of everything. You don't have to suddenly startle yourself by remembering, "Good Lord! I forgot to think about growing the left side of my hair last week, and now the right side is longer than the left!" Or, "I've been so busy for the last five minutes that I forgot to breathe!" and then have to stop and take copious gulps of air to catch up. No, you can be off having a marvelous time somewhere and the Little Man keeps you breathing and keeps your hair growing with no fuss and no muss to your Conscious thoughts.

The Sub-Conscious has another very interesting function. It stores away, for future reference, any information you have given it. Yes, *anything* and *everything* you have given it through the Conscious Mind has been stored away. See that little window there in the line between the two mind sections? Well, every time you have been impressed by something, you have taken it in through your eyes or your ears (or even through your mouth, if it's the taste of some marvelous lasagna you had last week!) and, once you've run it through the process in your Conscious Mind, it's passed through that window to the Little

Man, who takes it and files it away. Now, if you're kind of old-fashioned, you can imagine him back there with a row of filing cabinets. If you're modern, you can picture him with an IBM computer. Anyway, he takes this information and stores it in the proper place. He has taken everything—I repeat, *everything*—that you have ever learned, ever known, and has filed it back there. Even as you have read these words, what you have read has already been filed back into the Sub-Conscious.

It is important to realize that while the Little Man has filed things away, he doesn't automatically bring them back up and put them into your Conscious Mind. If he started giving you back all the information that you had given him since you were first a conscious being, can you imagine the confusion? This may be what happens when a person becomes senile and begins recalling events from the distant past as if they had happened yesterday. There seems to be a relaxing, with age, of the security measures that keep information from slipping back into the Conscious Mind.

But the important thing for you is to know that all these things *are* stored back there and that the Little Man will give you this information *if you ask*. He won't give anything to you that you don't ask for, though, because he has no originality. All he really knows is what you've given him, and all he can give you is what you've asked him to file away in the back. It won't do you a bit of good to ask him for Sophia Loren's private telephone number, because you (probably) never had it to give him in the first place.

The Little Man can be a very good friend, nevertheless, and will supply you with any information in the files providing you ask him in the proper way. That proper way has to be in the form of a command. He is your servant. He works for *you*. You have to command him for the information.

Let me give you an example of how this works. You are talking with a friend about a vacation trip you took together five years ago. You remember a marvelous little French restaurant where you were most impressed with the lobster bisque. "What was the name of that restaurant?" you ask your friend.

"I have it right on the tip of my tongue," the friend replies, adding, "We'll recall it in a minute."

"Yes," you reply, "it'll come to us." Then you change the

subject completely, talking about a television program of the night before. Suddenly, in the middle of this discussion, comes the name: "Mary Ann's Beer Joint!"

"Yes!" you exclaim. "*That* was the name of the French restaurant with the marvelous lobster bisque. Mary Ann's Beer Joint!"

This type of recall has happened to each one of us, and more than once. Trying without success to recall a name or a number, and then suddenly it comes charging into your thoughts when you had changed the subject.

What *really* happened? When you and your friend were on vacation, you were most impressed with this restaurant's food. So you said to each other, "We'll have to remember this place," and both of you sent back the name "Mary Ann's Beer Joint" to be filed away in your Sub-Conscious minds. Now you and your friend wanted the name of the place, but it was five years ago that you were there—five years ago, not right now—and therefore the name of the place was not in your *Conscious Minds* any longer.

You *give an order to your Little Man.* Phrases like "It'll come to us" and "We'll recall it" were used. The Little Man, surprised to get an order from you, quickly dropped the copy of *The Life Story of Raquel Welch in Seventeen Illustrated Volumes* that he'd been been reading and went over to the filing cabinets. Unsure how to proceed, he went to the "V" file to look under Vacation, then to the "H" file for Holiday, then to the "R" file for Restaurant, and finally over to the "F" file for Food, ending up in the subdivision marked Lobster Bisque. There was the name of the restaurant. Delighted, he came racing back to the little window, and even though you had changed the subject completely, he shouted: "MARY ANN'S BEER JOINT!"

Amazed to get this unexpected bit of news, you stopped short, listened, and then told your friend. It was that easy— and it works that way every time.

This is a simplified explanation of how your Sub-Conscious Mind works. Don't get too complicated. Don't start getting involved in the "how"s and "why"s. All you have to do right now is know—at a gut level—that it *does* work and that you can make it work for yourself. The first time you rode in an automobile you didn't wonder why it worked, but were just pleased that it did work. Then, if you had any technical inclinations at all, you might have looked into the mechanics of the car. Most of us, however, couldn't care less how a car works just so long as it takes us where we want to go. In this course we are dealing not with theories but with practicalities: not *why* a thing works, but *how* to make it *work for you*.

Your Little Man is an incredible servant. He is there only to work for you. He is not there to do the bidding of anyone else. For most of us, unfortunately, he hasn't been doing a lot of work because the majority of us don't ever *consciously* ask him to produce anything. Usually we're quite content to let him file away the names and the dates and the telephone numbers that come along, never *asking* him to produce any of them again. If we do, it's only accidental—as it was in the conversation about Mary Ann's Beer Joint.

Your Little Man is a very willing worker, but he's not very bright and sometimes he can be slow. Occasionally he'll even give you the wrong information, but your Conscious Mind will know it—you'll get that gut feeling—and send it back to him. Once you learn how to use him and once you start using him, you will be amazed how quickly he can come up with the information you ask for. But mostly he just sits there on a high stool reading *The Life Story of Raquel Welch in 17 Illustrated Volumes* and automatically filing away the information that comes through. The way to make him produce is to get him *used* to the idea of producing.

I want you to work a little now. I want you to think of someone in your past—I don't care how far back you want to go—someone whose name you can't remember, but whom you knew well at one time. It can be anyone at all whose name you've forgotten: a grade-school teacher whose name you can't remember; someone you worked with once, whose name you can't recall; someone you were married to once and have forgotten. It can be anyone, but it must be someone whose *first* and *last* names you once knew perfectly well and yet, even if I were to show you a photograph, you would not be able *consciously* to recall the names right now.

I want you to picture that person in the surroundings in which you knew him or her at that time. See the individual's face, see the place where you knew each other. Now give a *command* to your Little Man. Ask in a definite and commanding way for the name of this long-lost person. Make it a *positive* command, and say it *to yourself* three times:

"What was the name of the red-haired kid who sat beside me in seventh-grade history? What was the name of the red-haired kid who sat beside me in seventh-grade history? What was the name of the red-haired kid who sat beside me in seventh-grade history?"

*Ask it three times and then forget it!*

Change the subject. Get up and walk around. Look out of the window, read a book—do anything except think about that red-haired kid.

What will happen is that the Little Man, sitting alone back there, will be astounded that you have given him an order, and given it to him in such a forceful way. He will immediately drop whatever he's doing and rush to the filing cabinets.

You must leave him alone while he is looking for the answer. Don't keep repeating the command. Don't even think about it, for each time you do, the Little Man will come dashing back to the window to see what you want. And when he finds out it's the same order he'll just get flustered. Let the Little Man do his job without any interference from you.

If, after a few hours, he hasn't come up with the answer, then give the command again. Do this as many times as you choose until you get the answer, but don't confuse the Little Man by repetitions of the command in rapid succession.

If he should come up with the wrong answer, just to shut you up for a few minutes, refuse it and send it back. You'll know when the correct name has been given—you'll get that gut reaction. There will be a conscious acknowledgment that this is the correct name. I had one elderly woman student go back sixty-five years to come up with the name of a playmate from first grade. She was so startled by the rapidity and clarity of the answer that she burst into tears. I've had students recall important lost addresses, remember where they had hidden documents, and recall numbers of lost safety-deposit boxes.

I wish this technique was taught in schools today. Students wouldn't have to study so hard or cram themselves for examinations. All they would have to do would be to read the information and consciously file away the most important facts. Once they *knew* that the information was back there, their usual pre-exam tension would be greatly alleviated. So many aspects of your life can be improved just by using this simple procedure.

What does this have to do with psychic development? The technique we have been dealing with here is one of *activating* the Sub-Conscious Mind—activating it to the point at which it starts to heed your Conscious commands. In doing this, you open up a newer and straighter channel for the information you will receive from other levels of the mind and from the minds of *others*. But first you've got to get your Little Man working.

All this brings us to Figure 3.

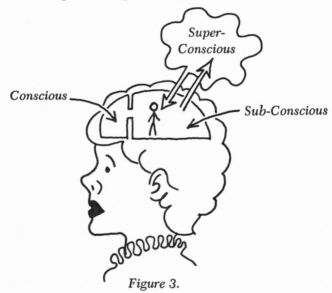

Figure 3.

There is a third mind level, apart and quite different from the Conscious and Sub-Conscious levels, that most of us are familiar with. This is the Super-Conscious—a rare, strange, almost unknown (and certainly uninvestigated) level of human ability. This is where it all happens. This is where everything originates: the creativity, the ideas, the ESP.

What do you think you are really saying when you tell someone, "I got an idea"? *Where* did you get it from? Was the five and ten having a "Summer Idea Sale? Did you walk down the street and notice an idea lying on the sidewalk? Of course not. You got an idea and it came from your Super-Conscious mind.

*The Super-Conscious is the creative force. All original ideas and inspirations come from it.*

This third level is not something I've invented, or something that was dreamed up in all the rush to sell occult books. This mind level has been mentioned by other writers and used by many groups all around the world throughout history. The Hawaiians knew about it; their Huna religion used it the same way that you are going to use it. The Australian aborigines talk quite openly about this third mind level and they use it for some rather startling telecommunication effects. The Indians in the Amazon and Matto Grosso jungles use it and frequently refer to it. Yogis use it. The Tibetans used it (and still do, even though the Chinese don't want them to). Even Madame Blavatsky knew about it and obviously used it in her theosophical writings and carryings-on.

For your psychic purposes, this mind level is the most important of the three you shall be using. This mind level *contains* all the answers. It *gives* all the answers. This is the one mediums, writers, artists, clairvoyants, inventors, you-name-it, use constantly when they are doing their particular thing.

If you talk to writers or artists, you'll invariably discover that when they are in the midst of creating, something seems to take them over and produces work *through* them. All good writers have times when entire pages are written through their fingers as they sit at the typewriter in amazement and watch the words pour out. A poet will think about a first line for an hour and then suddenly begin to scribble rapidly. When the pen stops, he finds that the poem has been completed, and he is just as surprised to see what's on the paper as if someone else had written it (which is perhaps the case). An artist will start out with an idea (there's that word again) and have a fixed notion of how he expects the finished painting to look. He starts applying the brush, and soon it takes on a life of its own, dashing here and there, adding colors and redefining old lines. The artist puts the brush down after an hour or more to find a totally different concept on his canvas but one that, nine times out of ten, is *better* than he had conceived through *conscious* planning. If you think I'm exaggerating, get *any* autobiography of

27

any *successful* artist or writer and you'll read this in his or her own words.

A few years ago an inventor in Chile came up with a plan for an automobile engine that didn't require pistons. As soon as the press announced it, an inventor in India said that he was working on the same thing, and another inventor in Austria said that *he* was working on the same thing too. These three men had somehow tuned into the same idea and had been given the same instructions. The Super-Conscious is a repository of universal knowledge. Anyone can tune into it and tap it. It is impartial and knows no national boundaries. It gives the knowledge freely to all those who ask.

As a writer, I've had the experience of submitting an idea for a book, only to be told by my publishers that they are doing a *similar* book by *another* writer. When this happens I usually wait—and sure enough, out comes a third book on the same theme by still *another* writer. We have all been given the same idea from the *same* source: the Super-Conscious Mind.

This extraordinary mind level (but then, they are *all* extraordinary) is supposed to contain all the information in the universe. All the great creative works, the great inventions, the great artistic inspirations and solutions to all future aspirations derive from it. It is the *world's* storehouse of knowledge and it makes the *Encyclopaedia Britannica* look like a Girl Scout pamphlet.

It contains everything you need to know. All you have to do is ask.

Let me show you how you have *already* used it.

You have a problem that needs a solution. You've cogitated and calculated, and you've wracked your brain (ah, but not your mind!), and still you can't come up with the solution. "What will I do?" you say to yourself. "I must have an answer by tomorrow. I must solve this problem by tomorrow." So you go to sleep, the solution still escaping you.

In the morning, you wake up and the first thing that pops into your head (see how the phrases we use reveal our instinctive knowledge of things? *Pops into your head* from where?) is the complete answer to your problem. You shout, "That's it!", jump out of bed and race off to put your newfound (where did you *find* it?) solution into practice.

Sounds familiar? Okay, then what did you *do?*

Quite simple. You asked the Little Man and he eventually gave you the answer. "But," you protest, "the answer was never in my Sub-Conscious. I never knew the answer, so how could I have filed it away back there?"

You didn't *ever* file it away. But your Little Man knew where to look!

Here's what happened. You searched your past experience on a conscious level for the solution to the problem. It wasn't there. Then you worried about it on a Sub-Conscious level. The Little Man had lots of time to search the records. It wasn't back there with him.

Then you became desperate. You had to have the answer by the next day. You told your Little Man in no uncertain terms that you *must* have the answer *in the morning*. Then you went to sleep. You stopped sending worrysome messages back to your Little Man and you gave him eight hours to find the solution.

He went through the files again. Still no answer back there. But when he couldn't come up with the answer, he then did an unusual thing: he sent a frantic telephone message up to the Super-Conscious.

"Hey!" he shouted. "I've got to have an answer to this problem or my boss will be in hot water tomorrow. He's really desperate. Please find the answer and send it back to me before he wakes up!"

The Super-Conscious went to work, pushed a few buttons, *easily* found the answer, then telephoned the Little Man and gave him the solution.

The Little Man sat up most of the night waiting for you to awaken. When you did, he shouted into your Conscious Mind: "The answer is X over Y equals C!" Once he was sure you had heard it and understood it, he went back to his corner, wiped his brow, and hoped to hell that the next time you needed an answer, you'd give him a little more time.

I've made this all sound very simple, but you need to understand the complicated mechanism of the mind levels on a simple ready-to-wear basis right now. Just know that it works and that this is *basically* the way it works. See for yourself.

Whenever you don't have the answer to something stored away in your Sub-Conscious, you can get it by giving your Little Man an *order* and a *time limit*. It is always best to give him a full night to work on it. While you are sleeping, you won't be demanding anything else and your bodily functions (which he must also attend to) are tuned to a low gear.

Creation, like mediumship, demands the blocking out of the Conscious Mind and the free flow of ideas *through* the Sub-Conscious *from* the Super-Conscious. It's vitally important for your psychic development that you understand this process, for everything you will do later depends on the unobstructed flow of information from the Super-Conscious. So, again, remember that the Conscious Mind must be blocked out long enough to receive information *through* the Sub-Conscious *from* the Super-Conscious.

Okay, work time. I want you to close your eyes and think of a problem that you want to solve. Now, don't make this problem the finding of a rich husband or a contract for a starring part in the next Robert Redford film, but a problem that has been bugging you that you've been unable to solve. A problem that *can* be solved—a problem that isn't earthshaking to anyone but yourself.

Now tell that problem to the Little Man. Tell him three times in a commanding way that you must have the answer, and give him a time limit: twenty-four hours will be fine, two days would be even better at this early stage. Tell him your problem in a definite sentence. *Tell him the problem but do not tell him how you want it solved. Just tell him to come up with the solution.* Don't tell him how to do his job or he will get confused and you'll never get the right answer. If *you* haven't been able, *consciously*, to come up with an answer yourself, you have no right to tell him how you want him to solve it. Just let him go and know he *will* solve it in the time limit you've given him.

Tonight, while you are in bed, tell him again. Repeat three times the problem and the fact that you need an answer. Then go to sleep and give him a chance to work. Expect to have the answer when you've asked for it to be given, and *listen for it when it is given.* That's very, very important. *Learn to listen when your Little Man gives you things.* Get out of the way of yourself and *listen*.

When I taught this class in Mexico City, one of the students was a wealthy and very charming lady who was having trouble with her son's expensive private school. The boy had failed an examination and had brought home a note telling her that he would fail the entire year. She wondered what was happening at the school because her son was bright and she was paying a fortune for his education. No amount of talking to her son would solve the problem and when she'd call, his teacher never seemed to be able to come to the phone. So she asked her Little Man to do something about it and to do it the next day.

That turned out to be a miserable rainy morning, and as she drove her boy and a neighbor's son to the school she heard the friend ask her son when he was going to give in and take the examination again. "*Can* you take it over?" she asked him quickly.

"I suppose I can," was the reply, "but I don't really want to. He tore up my last test paper before I could finish it."

"Aha!" she said to herself. "It's not that my son isn't bright, but there is a personality clash with the teacher. Now what, Little Man? Do I keep him in this school or transfer him to another one?"

As she drove into the yard of the school, the headmaster (a Jesuit priest) came out to her car. He stood there in the pouring rain and told her that, just a few minutes before, her son's teacher had come to him and said that he had irrationally torn up the boy's test paper and now wanted to give the child another chance. The priest, thinking all along that the trouble had been the boy's fault, hastened to apologize as soon as he saw the mother.

"I was stunned," she told the class later that day, "that the Little Man had worked so quickly to find the solution to my problem. As the priest stood there with the rain running down his face, I so wanted to tell him that my Little Man was making him do all this, but I didn't dare."

Another student, a surgeon in Texas, had a patient who needed a complicated operation on the nerves of one hand that had been horribly mutilated in an industrial accident. The surgeon wanted to save the hand, but didn't know how. On the eve of the operation (after he had searched all his medical books, to no avail) he turned the problem over to the Little Man. In the morning, the answer came pure and unadorned. It was something so simple that he had overlooked it. The operation was a success.

Now let's go from the mental to the physical. Not a *complete* jump, but rather to show you how the mental can affect the physical—in this case, your physical body.

# LESSON 3

# From Sickness Into Health

Work time, even before I get started with the explanation. I want you to sit comfortably in a chair, uncross your legs, and unclasp your hands. Now extend your right arm in front of you and open your hand. I want you to look at your palm, *really* look at it as if you had suddenly come across it in a box in the back of the closet and are fascinated by the discovery of this strange new thing. See the lines in it, see how it has mounds and hollows. Now stare at the very center of your palm. Stare at it, and as you stare I want you to imagine a circle in the center of your palm about the size of a quarter. A circle about the size of a quarter. Now stare at that circle. Stare at it. Concentrate on it.

As you do this I want you to imagine a flow of energy coming down your right arm and into your right palm. Feel it coursing down your right arm, through your wrist, and into the spot in the center of your palm. *Feel it.* Actually *see* it flowing with your inner vision.

As you do this, you'll feel the circle in your palm begin to tingle. It will start to get warm. It will begin to feel different from the area around it. Send the energy down your arm, into the circle in your palm. Feel the warmth. Feel the new sensation. *Concentrate upon that circle and keep concentrating on it until it begins to tingle or grow warm.*

When you feel this—*really feel it*—extend your left hand and feel the difference between the two palms. For some of you the difference may be slight, for others there will be considerable difference—but *there will be a difference!*

What have you done? You have given the Little Man in your Sub-Conscious an order to send energy into your palm. You have commanded him to send that energy until you could feel it, and he has obeyed your command. Your *mental* efforts have caused a *physical* change in your body. You have taken the first step that the yogis took who are able to control their heartbeats, their blood pressure, and their pain centers. You have taken the first step toward complete mastery over your physical body.

The mind is an incredible energy tool and the more we learn about it, the more fascinating it becomes. It will do whatever you ask it to do—even make you ill. This sort of thing happens to all of us sometimes. For example, you are dashing around the house getting ready to go someplace in a hurry when the phone rings. Quickly you pick it up. It's Mary on the other end.

"Hello, Sue? Mary. Listen, I want you to come to a party tomorrow night at my place. My sister is here from Detroit with her new husband and I know you're dying to see her again."

"Well," you say, "I really don't know if ——"

"Oh, you must come! It wouldn't be any fun without you."

"Look, can I call you back? I was just leaving the ——"

"Can't wait, Sue dear, I've got to tell the caterers how many to expect. Please say you'll come."

Finally, to get rid of her you say okay, you'll be there. Then you hang up. You are furious with Mary, but even more furious with yourself for not having the guts to tell her you really don't want to go to her dumb party. You've met the sister before and you haven't liked her and you certainly don't want to spend the evening with a man stupid enough to marry her. "Why didn't I say no?" you ask yourself. "I don't want to go to that party! I wish there was some way I could get out of it! I wish I could think up an excuse for not going tomorrow night!"

The next day, you awaken with a sore throat and a headache. You gargle and take an aspirin, but nothing seems to help. As the day grows so do your pains. Finally you pick up the phone.

"Hello, Mary? Listen dear, I have a terrible headache and a sore throat so I just can't come to your party tonight. I'm terribly sorry because I would have loved to see your sister and her husband. Oh, you do understand? Thank you, love. Good-bye."

You hang up and now what happens? Within a few minutes of getting out of the party, you find that your sore throat has vanished, along with your headache. You feel marvelous.

What has happened? The Little Man again. You did not want to go to that party. You told him that you wanted an excuse for not going and you gave him a night to come up with one. He did. He gave you the sore throat and the throbbing head, *and as soon as they had served your purpose, he took them away.* Now don't laugh, for you've done this to yourself time and time again without really knowing it.

If you stop and think a minute, you'll probably be able to name any number of friends who do the same thing, but probably don't realize what they're doing. In Brazil, I had a very good friend who was always looking for work. He was young, good-looking, and personable, but whenever he took a job it seemed he would become ill and have to leave it. I pulled a few strings with the president of Brazil's biggest airline and got him a job as flight steward. He was delighted to wear a fancy uniform and fly all over the country—but he didn't like having to serve passengers their drinks and food trays. That, he told me, reduced him to the level of a common waiter. (South Americans can be very class conscious.) So one day he noticed small blisters appearing between his fingers. They grew larger and became filled with a yellow fluid until he finally couldn't use his hands at all.

The airline gave him a month's sick leave and during that time he must have visited every doctor in Rio. I took him to five that I knew myself. But at the end of the month, his hands were worse and, so, because he could no longer serve customers, the airline fired him. What happened then? You guessed it! Within three days, the boils vanished and his hands returned to normal!

He had wanted the money, the prestige, and the chance to travel, but he rebelled against serving people—so strongly that his Little Man took him at his word and created a condition where he would not be able to do so. When I tried to show him that he had brought it all on himself, he became furious with me. The origin couldn't have been mental because the boils were quite *physical,* he said. It was the end of our friendship.

Mind over matter. You know something? It works.

The American Medical Association has stated in its *Journal* that 78 percent of all patients who go to doctors are suffering from psychosomatic illnesses—78 percent!! In other words, mind-induced afflictions brought on in much the same way as Sue's headache and sore throat. (Unfortunately, while the medical profession recognizes the ailments as *mental,* it treats them *physically,* with injections, pills, and scalpels.)

Many people use illness as a crutch. It's the only way they can get sympathy or attention. Watch the little old lady who gets on the bus carrying a cane. Everyone moves aside for her; a gentleman rises and gives up his seat for the poor dear. Watch her at the store counter and see how others defer to her because she needs a cane. But get her to cure herself and throw away that cane? Never! That cane gives her the attention she craves. She doesn't want to walk normally. Normal means she is just one more dog in the pack.

We learn this early. Remember how you could always get attention from your mother, even when she was busy washing clothes or cooking dinner, if you went crying to her with a hurt or a bee sting, either real or imagined? She stopped what she was doing, kissed it, and "made it well." You felt much better for the love and attention, and even if the hurt had been real, somehow it actually was much better after that kiss. Your mother wasn't dispensing penicillin or iodine with her kiss, but for some reason it worked medical wonders all the same, for your Little Man had already been instructed that mommy's kiss would make everything well.

Now, if the mind can make you sick, it follows that it can also make you well. Correct? If the energies of your Little Man can be channeled toward illness, they can also be channeled toward health. For instance, I have a wonderful mother who is almost never ill. When I was a child in those awful Ohio winters, everyone in the family would have a cold. Not Mom. "I don't have time for a cold," she would say, and she'd never come down with one. Other people became ill and asked her to come care for them. "I don't have time to get ill," and off she'd go to help someone and never fall ill herself. After a while I finally realized what she was doing (I'm a slow learner!), and when I would feel myself coming down with a sore throat or a pain in my back I'd say, "Oh, no you don't! I don't have time for that!" and in a few minutes the soreness or the pain would be gone.

Once the Little Man in your Sub-Conscious gets an order, he'll carry it out. He can do other things besides getting rid of headaches and minor pains.

Another friend of mine once noticed a large lump forming under the skin inside his leg near the groin. When it became red and hard he went to a doctor, who told him it would have to be operated upon. Not wanting any knife to cut him open, he returned home and gave an order to his Little Man. "Get rid of that thing on my leg. You know how it built up, so take it away in the same manner." He said it once or twice a day and then went about his normal business. "A few days later," he recalled, "when I was taking a shower, I remembered the lump and looked down to see how it was. I couldn't find it. It had vanished."

The next time you have an ache or a pain or are just feeling lousy in general, take a few minutes and give a stern command to your Little Man. Tell him you do *not* want to be sick, that there are things you must do that day, and that since he knows how this built up in your body, he also knows how to take it away. Order him to make you well, and he will make you well.

Of course, if your ailment has been inside your body festering for several years, don't expect one or two commands to get rid of it instantly. It may happen that way, but the chances of it are slim. Nature works in gradual ways. In an extreme condition, you must expect to eliminate your affliction gradually. Be persistent because in nature's way, persistence pays off. But your Little Man can cure almost any ailment—even, according to several doctor friends I have, cancer.

I believe, and so do many medical doctors, that the majority of all illnesses are caused by the mind. People give themselves their sicknesses. Of course, you'll argue that you would never give yourself a tumor or arthritis, yet when there is no way for the negative energies you take into your mind and body to escape, they build up inside you and create an imbalance. This imbalance eventually manifests itself as an illness—a physical illness. Medical men agree that an ulcer can be caused by *mental* anguish. The problems that well up inside the mind create the abcess in the stomach. Yet this *mental* negative energy can form into a *physical* effect that can be X-rayed, seen with the naked eye, and removed by physical surgery.

You don't have to want an illness. *It can form inside you because you haven't released the negative thoughts and emotions* that you've stored away with your Little Man. If he doesn't know what to do with them he will channel them to a weak part of your body and create a physical imbalance. Why doesn't he remove this negativity? Because he takes orders directly from you. You have given him this negative energy but you *haven't* told him to throw it away. He hangs onto it and uses it because you did not tell him otherwise.

Look at the word "disease." It is, in reality, "dis" and "ease." An imbalance of ease, i.e. an unsettling influence. Sickness!

Let me tell you the story of a lady I'll call Helen. She was very much into the psychic and metaphysics. She was a professional decorator in a large city and very good at what she did. But she was married to a real louse and they had two beautiful children. She would have left him, but she worried about her kids. He left her one day, and with no thoughts as to what would happen to the children. Helen, stunned by his walking out, searched for pity from her friends.

None of us gave her any. In fact, we unanimously agreed that she was better off without him. But Helen began to worry about life without "a man" to protect her and pay the bills. (He hadn't been outstanding on either count.) She became ill, her mother took in the children, and her doctor ordered her into the hospital. There, on the operating table, the surgeons found that Helen had seven cancerous tumors. They sewed her back up and told her that she had six months to live.

Helen spent about a day feeling sorry for herself, when suddenly she remembered how much she loved her children and how much they needed her. She remembered her loathesome husband, and then she became determined. She'd show him and the world that she was strong enough to go it alone, and to hell with any man. In three days she dismissed herself from the hospital, moved to a new town, took a steady job, and began an entirely new life.

When the six months were up, she wasn't dead. When a year was up she went back to see her doctor. He ran some tests. All the cancers had disappeared! Her body was clean and healthy.

I asked her what she had done, because I knew it had all been accomplished on a mental level.

"I got out of that hospital bed and I looked at myself in the mirror and I said to myself, 'Okay, let's cut this out. I have no intention of dying. My children need me and I have a full life ahead. I don't know how those cancers got in there, but you do. So get rid of them the same way you built them up!' I told my Little Man that every day, several times a day. Then I forgot about it because I *knew* he would take care of it." He did.

Dr. Carl Simonton is one of the few medical doctors in the United States who is using the power of the mind to heal. He does this in a fascinating and highly successful way. The only patients he will take are terminal cases, persons who have been told by their doctors that they are dying of cancer and have no hope. He "reprograms" these people, he does not use medicines, cobalt treatment, surgery. All he does is get them into contact with their Sub-Conscious and teach them to *re-think* their problems, thus changing the message that their mind sends to their body. He has a batting average of something like 85 percent success. In other words, eighty-five out of every hundred terminally ill cancer patients *live! Without* their cancers. He has refined to the $n$th degree the premise I've been showing you here: "I don't have time to be ill."

# LESSON 4

# The Cosmic Forces

Once in every lifetime a person is given an absolute truth. It is often something so simple that it is ignored. Such a truth was given to me. I ignored it. Then, miraculously, it was given to me again. This time I understood it for what it was and accepted it. I consider it one of the most important metaphysical realities I have ever encountered.

The second time it was given, I was told that I had the liberty of telling everyone I knew about it, but they had the liberty to refuse it if it did not register upon them the way it did on me. Now I want to give it to you, for what it's worth to you. There is a time for everything, even psychic guidance. For your sake I hope that *now* is your time.

In Brazil, in the southern state of Rio Grande do Sul, there was a medium, a marvelous, almost illiterate black woman. I had met her when I was researching my book *Drum & Candle* and still consider her one of the most amazing psychics I've ever met. She told me things about myself that were uncanny, things even I had forgotten. She also told me things that would happen in the future (a more dangerous area for a medium to wander in), and *everything* she predicted came true. I have never found another psychic able to do that and I've interviewed them and had readings with them all across the United States, into Mexico, across Great Britain, and even down into South Africa. Dona Leda Simonele of Brazil is simply superb.

Dona Leda was the only child of a Brazilian father and a Paraguayan Indian mother. When she was very young, her father left to live with another woman and Leda's mother had to take in washing to support the two of them. When Leda was four years old she saw a strange, tall man, his skin bronzed from the sun, walk across the floor of their wooden shack and go out into the backyard. He smiled at Leda as he rested against a tree. Leda ran to a neighbor's house, where her mother was working, and told her about the strange man. Her mother came running back with the child but couldn't see anyone. "There he is," Leda insisted, "against the tree."

Still her mother couldn't see him, and she was so angry that Leda had taken her away from her work that she locked her in the bedroom for the rest of the afternoon. When her mother returned, she said she'd open the door only if Leda promised not to tell lies like that again. The child agreed. The door was opened and Leda looked into the backyard. "Mama," she said,

"I'm sorry, but the man is still there." Her mother couldn't see him, and Leda went back into the bedroom.

Once, on a rainy day, Leda went with her mother to deliver a basket of clean clothes. They were walking on the railroad tracks and Leda was told to step on the wooden ties and not on the ground so as not to get her shoes dirty. Then, coming down the tracks toward them, Leda saw a little girl about ten years old, wearing a fancy white party dress with lots of ribbons and ruffles—but it was muddied and torn. "Mama," Leda asked, "how come that white girl is allowed to get dirty and I'm not?" Her mother couldn't see any white girl and told Leda to stop being silly. But the girl kept coming closer and closer and finally, when the girl seemed about to bump into her, Leda jumped off the tracks and into the mud. The girl passed right on by, through Leda's mother. Furious that Leda had muddied her shoes, her mother refused to hear anything about some white girl in a pretty dress making her do it. Years later, Leda learned that a young white girl had run away from a party wearing a white dress with lots of ribbons and ruffles. She had been killed on those train tracks, right about where Leda had seen her ghost.

Soon after this incident, someone gave Leda a deck of ordinary playing cards and she discovered that she could tell people things about themselves whenever she spread the cards for them. "There is a little voice in my head," she explained to me, "and all I have to do is listen to it. I don't know if it's a man's or a woman's voice. It sounds like one of those old-fashioned Gramophone records." One day when Leda was about ten years old, a teen-age neighbor girl came calling with her brother and asked for her fortune to be told. The voice told Leda that the girl was pregnant. "What's pregnant mean?" she asked the teen-ager, "because that's what you are." The girl was so furious that she slapped Leda's face and stormed home.

That evening the girl's mother came to Leda's house and demanded she be punished for spreading wicked gossip about her daughter. Leda was punished and her mother burned her cards. A month later the neighbor girl wasn't feeling well and went to a doctor. He told her she was pregnant. She was only fifteen and thought babies were produced by kissing. There was an older neighbor boy who was having regular sex with her . . . but she'd never allowed him to kiss her.

I could go on for pages about Leda and things she has told people that have come true. The most memorable, of course, to me, are the ones she predicted for me.

I had finished researching *Drum & Candle* and was going to leave Brazil. There had been a revolution and the military mob was worse than any leftist dictatorship. Friends were being jailed, others taken from their homes and never heard of again. My own apartment had been ransacked by the military goons because I had been friends with the former President and his lovely First Lady. So I had decided to return to the States and take a job in New York. I went to see Leda for the last time.

After I told her my plans she looked at me and said, "Are there palm trees in New York?" She, who had never been out of southern Brazil, had no idea what New York was or probably even *where* it was. "No," I said, "there aren't."

"You are going to go where there are palm trees and you're going to write another book."

I told her that there were no palm trees in Manhattan and I was certainly not going to write another book. I had had it with the uncertainties of being an author. I wanted a steady job with steady hours and, most important, a steady salary. She shook her head. "No, you are going to go where there are palm trees and you're going to write another book."

I left her tiny apartment that afternoon quite saddened. For one thing, I knew I probably would never see her again; and for another, she had been so wrong with my last reading! Before, everything she had predicted had come true, but now it looked as if Leda was losing her touch.

Well, to make a long story short, I went to New York and was offered a *magnificently* high-paying job to write for the company magazine of an international corporation. But one week before I was to start, the stock market fell and the corporation's shares tumbled along with everyone else's on Wall Street. (That was in April 1970 for any of you who remember.) Obviously, the last thing this stunned company needed was another writer!

I stayed on in New York for a full six weeks looking for a job, but there were none to be had. Nobody needed a writer. Then a friend of mine called. She was Maggie Anthony, a tarot reader and a darned good one at that. She lived in San Francisco and had an enormous house. Why didn't I come out there and get a job? There was lots of work and I could stay in her house until I found a place of my own. Great idea! I took the last of my money, bought an airline ticket, and flew out to San Francisco. But (why is there always a "but"?) when I got there I discovered that everyone who couldn't find a job in New York was looking for one in San Francisco. So after a day of pounding the pavements, I'd drop into the shop where Maggie gave her readings and go home with her.

Because of my psychic investigations in Brazil I had become interested in finding out what was happening on the California psychic scene, which seemed to be the most active of any in the States. What I hoped to do was buy a book about it and go to see some of the people listed in it. I went into a shop and asked the clerk for such a book. "There isn't any," she told me. Sure that the clerk didn't know what she was talking about, I went into another book shop. "No," the clerk said, "there isn't such a book. But there should be."

You know those cartoons in which a man gets an idea and a light bulb over his head goes "boing"? Well, my light bulb went on with a loud "boing" as I heard those words: there should be. I went across the street to a pay phone and called my editor in New York—collect of course. By the time he came to the phone, I had worked out a complete outline of a book about the California occult scene. He liked it, told me to send him a written proposal, and within one week, I had a signed contract and several thousand dollars in my pocket for a book, *The Psychic World of California*.

The first person I interviewed was a medium in San Jose, who picked me up at the bus station and drove me to her home for the interview. As we went, she pointed out some of the historic parts of the city. "You see those palm trees?" she asked. "It was a tradition that every settler would plant a palm tree in his front yard."

Here I was in a place where there were palm trees and writing another book! *Dona Leda had been right.*

This incident continues to puzzle me. How did this semiliterate black woman in the tip end of Brazil *know* that I would end up in California writing another book? How did she *know* this a good eight months before it happened and when I, at my last meeting with her, was positive in my own mind that I was going to live and work in New York City? I wish our scientists would get busy and start researching this line of energy instead of the hundred and fifty thousand silly things they are poking into now. Ah, but there is no profit in psychic research. It isn't commercial, it isn't salable to the average consumer. So . . . there's no money for research. Aren't you glad you live in an enlightened society and not in some greedy backward culture interested only in material things?

When I was with Dona Leda, she told me about *As Forças Cosmicas* and said that her guides had given her permission to give me the information. I smiled, copied it down, and promptly forgot all about it because it was too "quaint" to really work.

Then I started my research into *The Psychic World of California* and met a tiny big-hearted lady named Dottie Vurnovas. Dottie lived in a mobile home in San Jose and had a following of faithful friends and clients who sang her praises wherever I went. She bowled me over with her charm and amazed me with her naturally developed psychic abilities. I once had a friend in Ohio, suffering from a skin rash that was sending her to the hospital the next day, telephone Dottie in California and Dottie sent her healing energies over the wires. As she listened to Dottie, my friend turned beet red, began to perspire and shake. The next morning the rash was gone, the hospital appointment canceled. (I later devoted a full chapter to Dottie in my book *Psychic Healers*.)

Anyway, during one of my frequent visits to Dottie's trailer she gave me a formula. "My guides say it's all right for you to have it, and you may even publish it if you choose. You will be able to reach many more people with it through your books and your classes. Of course," she added, "those who understand it will accept it. Those who don't, simply won't."

I listened to the formula in open-mouthed astonishment, for it was the very same Cosmic Forces formula that Dona Leda had given me in Brazil some three years before. I've never seen it published anywhere. I've never heard anyone else using it except these two mediums at opposite ends of the globe who knew about it and were "told" in different languages to give it to me. I will now give it to you:

Stand with your feet slightly apart and your arms down at your sides but *not touching* your body. Take a deep breath and as you breathe in, say *to yourself:*

"I bring the Cosmic Forces into my body"—here hold your breath—then continue, *to yourself,* "asking for Strength, Protection, and Guidance." Exhale. Do it two more times.

Simple. Free. Extraordinarily effective. Let's examine it.

We talked earlier about radio waves and energies running through the air that you cannot see or taste. In this exercise you literally turn yourself into a receptacle (a radio, if you want to think that way) that *captures* a special spiritual wavelength and turns on your "machinery."

By standing and relaxing and breathing in deeply you are plugging yourself into the current just as truly as if you were plugging a radio into an electrical socket. You repeat the formula three times and by the third time you will have *tuned in* to the right channel for you. If you think of yourself as a radio plugging in and tuning in, it will come into you much faster.

And it does come into you! Make no mistake about it. You will *feel* the force. Many people find that it shakes their body or gives them a sensation of falling over. (These sensations diminish after a few times but in the beginning can be a little surprising.)

I want you also to think of what you are asking for: Strength, Protection, and Guidance. (I put them in capital letters because they are too important to be relegated to lower case.)

What do the words *Strength . . . Protection . . . Guidance* mean to *you?* I want you to shut this book, close your eyes, and think about those three words and their meaning. Once you've done this, open your eyes and let's continue.

*Strength.* Suppose you had a neighbor who was always there when you needed him. You feel weak, alone, unsure whether or not you can continue. You doubt your own abilities, your own talents. So you go to this neighbor and tell him your problems and he gives you the *strength* you need to go on.

*Protection.* You are afraid. The world is too vast, you are too tiny inside it. Your ambitions seem that of a lion, yet you are only an ant. You go to your neighbor and he gives you the *protection* you seek.

*Guidance.* You are unsure where to go, how to get there, and what to do if you do get there. Should you take this path or that? Should you trust this person or that one? Should you take this job, make this trip, marry that person? You go to this same neighbor and he gives you the *guidance* you need.

That would be one helluva neighbor to have, right?

Well, you have such neighbors and they are right next to you. All you have to do is plug in and tune in and they'll be there without fail all the time. The beautiful thing about the Cosmic Forces is that *you are never alone.* Whether on a mountaintop or in the middle of a crowded city, with the Cosmic Forces to guide you, you are *never* alone. That fact in itself makes this formula more valuable than a king's ransom.

Now let's do this in stages. Don't rush through it just to get it done. Let's do it correctly each time so that you will have it correctly filed away by the Little Man back there. (No, I haven't forgotten about him. He plays an important part in this formula, as you will see.)

Stand up, put your feet slightly apart, your hands down at your sides but not touching your body. Also make sure that you are not touching another person or a chair or a piece of furniture. I don't want your body to have any outside sensations. The force of the Forces is what I want you to experience.

Let's practice saying the formula now. This is just practice for the first real time. You must *know* the words and *understand* their meaning. Repeat after me:

*I bring the Cosmic Forces into my body, asking for Strength, Protection, and Guidance.*

Repeat it as many times as necessary until you have memorized the formula.

Now, still standing, close your eyes and take a deep breath. Say, *to yourself, "I bring the Cosmic Forces into my body"* — here hold your breath—and continue, to *yourself, "asking for Strength, Protection, and Guidance."* Exhale.

Say it again.

Repeat it for the third time.

Open your eyes.

What did you *feel?* Did you feel something running into your body? Some electricity? Some new sensation? Did you think you were about to fall either forward or backward? Did you get a tingling in your spine, your face, your hands?

Now let's do it again, but this time with a few additions— *important* additions.

The reason for calling in the Cosmic Forces in the first place is because you want something, right? You need something, you want something done, you have a request. "They" understand that and that's what "they" are there for. "They" come when you call on them because "they" want to help you. "They" are with you. You are never alone, so don't be backward or ashamed about asking them to do things for you. Of course, you must use some discretion in what you ask. Don't expect them to commit murder for you or help you rob your neighbor of his wife.

Which brings up an interesting point: Make sure you *really* want what you are asking for. Once you get it, in this way, you are stuck with it. Do you *really* want that man in your office to fall in love with you? Do you really want your ex-wife back? Consider your requests carefully. They are easier to get than to get rid of.

Decide what you want to ask for this first time around. It can be anything: love, a new job, help in your career, health for yourself, a new car, whatever.

This time, *after you have said the formula three times,* you can breathe normally and make your request.

When you do this, be natural about it. Just because you are talking to unseen forces is no reason for you to phrase your question, "Oh please, thou most greatest of intellects, bestow thy knowledge on me, this humble seeker after truth." They will probably tell you to cut out the fanciness and talk naturally. They know you. They've heard you in conversation and inside your thoughts. You won't get anywhere any faster by pouring on the holier-than-thou oil.

Take as long as you want on your request, but make sure it is exactly phrased. If it's a problem that you've been unable to solve, tell "them" about it and ask them to give you a solution. Again, as with the Little Man, don't tell them how to solve it. Just ask them to solve it. (If *you* knew how to solve it, it wouldn't be a problem, right?) Then, once you have phrased your question, conversed with the Forces, cross your arms over your chest like an Egyptian mummy, say "Thank you, thank you, thank you," and sit down.

The reason for the crossing of the arms, where they form an "X" over your breast, right palm open on left upper arm and left palm open on right upper arm, is that you are turning off the energy. First you plugged in and tuned in; now that you are done with the energy, you turn it off (as you would turn off a radio when you were through listening to it) and this Egyptian "double-cross" seems the best way to do it.

The reason for saying "Thank you" is obvious. You've asked for a personal favor, maybe a colossal favor if it's granted, and you should have the good manners to say thanks for it. It is also a way of showing your appreciation for what the Forces are going to do for you—and for what they have done for you in the past—and also a sign of humility. (A rare commodity in this day and age!) Then too, for some reason "they" like to be thanked. They like to hear it. I suppose it makes them feel good. In all religions and rituals, the world over, man is always *thanking* God, Shiva, Jesus, Mohammed, or Buddha for what he has been given or what he is about to receive. The Cosmic Forces like to hear it too. Remember that. (Also remember to *really* thank them when they come through on your request!)

The Cosmic Forces are many things to many people. If you want to look at them as "God," then do it. If you want to think of them as "Spirit," then that is the way you should think of them. I prefer to think of the Cosmic Forces as "Intelligent Energy" with no names, no personality, but with infinite wisdom, patience, and love. I feel you are limiting yourself if you think of the Cosmic Forces as *one* entity or one individual. They say in the Bible that God is everywhere and in everything all the time. That's how I see the Forces: always here, always ready to listen and always ready to act in our behalf.

The Cosmic Forces differ from the Super-Conscious in that they are separate and apart from all human control and influence. While we are all connected with the Super-Conscious, the Cosmic Forces are not bound to anyone or anything. They just *are*. I like to think of them as *supplying* the Super-Conscious with information, aiding the Super-Conscious in its search for information. The Super-Conscious *is*. The Cosmic Forces *are*. Both exist to help us and for that we say thank you, thank you, thank you!

Now, after the request and the thanks, *listen*. You ask for advice, you ask for help, and then you *listen* to what is given to you. It might not be given instantly. It might take a few hours or even a few days for the answer to come via the Super-Conscious, but *be prepared to stop and listen* to it whenever and wherever it comes.

Then, finally, *act*. It doesn't do a damned bit of good to get information if you don't do anything with it. That next-door neighbor we were talking about will be glad to give you advice time after time. But once he sees that you aren't following his advice, that you are going out and doing what you had planned to do anyway before you took up his valuable time, he won't be so anxious to continue helping you. As a matter of fact, after a while he won't even come to the door when you knock. And you can't blame him.

The Cosmic Forces work the same way. They are not going to use their energies time after time. If you don't pay any attention to them once you ask them for help, they'll say "forget it" and be off helping someone who's more appreciative.

The uses of these Cosmic Forces are legion, but one that I heartily recommend is the White Light for daily protection. I'm always getting people who ask me how they can protect themselves from evil, witchcraft, negativity, jealousy, and so on. And almost always I tell them to start their day with the Cosmic Forces and White Light exercises, as follows.

In the morning, after you've bathed and gotten dressed and are ready to leave the house to go out into that big wicked world lurking outside your door, do the Cosmic Forces exercise. Plug in and tune in three times, make your request or give thanks for some recently received favor. Then raise your hands palm upward, as if you were wondering if it was sprinkling on a summer day, and ask the Cosmic Forces to protect you with the White Light.

As you ask, visualize this light coming down and into you. How you see it is your own doing. Some people like to see the light coming down over them like an upside-down ice cream cone (but without the chocolate or vanilla, please!). Others see it coming down like a single shaft of light, or laser beam, entering their foreheads or the top of their heads. Still others see it as a white mist enveloping their bodies, while others see themselves standing in a circular smooth tube of white light.

I see it as white smoke starting at the floor around my feet and then coming up my body as if I were being wrapped in the stuff like a mummy. When it gets to the top of my head, I mentally tie a knot in it and close it off. Sometimes, when I am going out on an especially difficult day, I'll bring the light up twice, giving myself double protection at no extra cost.

You will know when this White Light has enveloped you because you'll feel a tingling in the palms of your hands. Stand there until you feel the tingling and then visualize the protective light in whatever way you wish. Then, when you are well covered, cross your arms in the Egyptian double-cross and say, "Thank you, thank you, thank you."

You are now able to go out into the world and know that you are protected from all the negativity, maliciousness, and confusion that bombard every one of us constantly. Spiritists claim that if you have given yourself this protective coating, nothing can penetrate it and hurt you. Negativity (I prefer that word to "evil") will hit the White Light and bounce off.

Interestingly enough, this is basically what the voodoo priests prescribe for persons who think they have been "cursed." They get the victims to place the white protective light around themselves, telling them that whoever is sending the evil will receive it back twice as hard. The theory is that the negativity is sent flying at you, hits that invisible shield and bounces off with twice the force, returning on the same wavelength that sent it—that of your enemy. You don't even have to know who is sending the negativity toward you. The negative power will dash back right along the path it came.

I once did a bit of research in Brazil on voodoo priests and priestesses. Those who were practicing white (good) magic lived to ripe old ages. Of those involved in black (negative) magic, almost all were dead before they reached middle age. One black-magic lady in the city of São Paulo had a very lucrative practice in which she would kill off enemies for a sizeable hunk of cash. Someone would come to her and give her the name of the person he wanted eliminated. Then she would turn on her shortwave radio and listen to the police broadcasts of accidents and deaths. As soon as she heard of a fatal accident and heard the victim's full name being reported, she would go into her routine and contact the poor troubled spirit who had just lost his body and didn't know what to do. "You will find your way to your destination if you'll take the spirit of John So-and-so," she would say, giving the ghost the name of the person her client wanted eliminated.

Spirit would go get spirit, the client would have his satisfaction, she would have her money. But one day when she was working on a "case," instead of saying the name of a future victim, she made a mistake and said the name of her only son. Shocked at what she had done, she tried desperately to undo it. Too late! That very afternoon her son "fell" under the wheels of a truck and was killed instantly. True story—it's in the Brazilian police files.

The above is a good reason why you should think twice about using any psychic technique for a negative purpose. Down through the ages and through the various religions and cults, the sender of evil always ran the risk of having it come back in his own face if the prospective victim has protected himself in any way. If the victim is unaware and wide open, then zap!—he gets it. But if the victim knows something is wrong and has taken the trouble to fortify his aura with positive energy, then zap!—right back to the sender.

It is very important that you really perfect your Cosmic Forces exercise. It should be done until it becomes automatic, because later on, you're going to use it in many different ways—in healing, in contacting anyone anywhere in the world, in convincing somebody to hire you or buy your product. It is one of the most valuable tools I've ever learned, and I can't understand how I managed to survive as long as I did without it!

# LESSON 5

# On Falling Asleep

The majority of us have trouble falling asleep at night. I used to, but since I learned the technique, I'm going to teach you in this chapter. I sleep well and wake up refreshed.

There was a time when I used to go to bed at night completely exhausted and fall asleep almost at once. I'd sleep for about an hour and then—ping! I'd be wide awake thinking of all the things I had to do the next day, and all the problems that needed solving in the next few weeks. I'd try to shut out these thoughts, but when you're lying there in the dark with no place to look except inward, it isn't easy. (I even tried counting sheep a few times, but they turned into problems jumping over a fence and so the hell with it.) After punching the pillow and telling myself to go to sleep, I'd get up and take a sleeping pill. Of course the pill did nothing but leave a bad taste in my mouth, and so in about another hour I'd get up and take another pill, this time washed down with a healthy belt of bourbon. Oh, I slept after that, but when I woke in the morning my head was two sizes larger than it normally is, and my tongue felt as if a team of midgets had been playing football on it. I looked for an easier way, and I found it.

No matter how exhausted your body is, your *mind* must also be willing to settle down for the night. The Little Man must be told to punch his time clock, hang up his apron, and turn in. You must convince your Sub-Conscious to relax and then your Conscious Mind will not be subjected to that all-night bombardment that so many of us know only too well.

The easiest and best method I've found is to go down to your relaxation level (or your Alpha level, as some people are calling it). The Alpha level runs your body at a different rate of speed, slows down your heartbeat, and can even affect your blood pressure. There are many books on the Alpha level if you care to read them. Here, we are not interested in *why* it works but in *how* it can work for you.

The technique you're going to learn works with colors, through a simple basic color progression. Let's get started.


## RED

I want you to close your eyes and visualize the color *Red*. It can be a *Red* anything—a red rose, a red carnation, a red apple, a man in a red Santa Claus suit, the inside of a watermelon;

anything that is *Red*. I want you to actually *see* this *Red* color inside your mind. I want that flash of *Red* to be there inside you. I don't care if it doesn't remain and just flits in and out for a particle of a second. The important thing is that you actually *see* the *Red* color inside your head.

Once you have seen it then go *down* to the next color, which is:

## ORANGE

I want you to visualize the color *Orange*. Bring that color into your mind and actually *see* it there. *See Orange:* a mound of fresh oranges piled high in a supermarket, a freshly poured glass of orange juice, a Buddhist monk in an orange robe. Use whatever you need to visualize the color, but *see* the color *Orange* in your mind's eye.

When you have it, let's go *down* to the next color, which is:

## YELLOW

I want you to visualize the color *Yellow*. Actually see it inside your head. If necessary, picture a yellow egg yolk in the center of a white plate, the yellow center of a daisy, the yellow sun burning in a clear sky. I want you to actually *see* the color *Yellow*.

When you have it, then go *down* to the next color, which is:

## GREEN

I want you to visualize the color *Green* in your mind's eye. Choose what you need to make it come into you: a freshly mown green lawn, the green leaves of a full tree in spring, a plant with large leafy green leaves, the Irish shamrock. Use whatever you need to *see* the color *Green* inside your head.

When you have it, I want you to go *down* to the next color, which is:

## BLUE

I want you to visualize the color *Blue*. Take whatever object you need to bring blue into your mind's eye—a bright blue sky without a cloud in sight, the blue of the ocean, the blue of a lake stretching far in the distance. Use whatever you need, but you must *see* the color *Blue.*

When you have it, let's go *down* to the next color, which is:

## LILAC OR VIOLET

Here you have a little more leeway. You can choose either *Lilac* or *Violet:* a lilac bush all in thick bloom, the delicate blossoms of a potted violet, a mist of lilac smoke curling around you. Use whatever you need but you must *see* the color *Lilac* or *Violet.*

Once you have done that, you are at your Alpha level. It's as simple as that. No fuss, no muss, no aftertaste.

Should you have trouble picturing any of the above colors find something around you that is that color, stare at it, and then close your eyes and try to reproduce that object with its color in your mind. After just a few tries you'll find it easy, and soon the colors will come just as flashes to you without taking the shape of the objects you started concentrating on. For some reason the color red seems to be the biggest hangup for most people. Others find it difficult to find a true violet or lilac for themselves. But it can be done, is painless and harmless—and it works.

Here's how to make it work.

When nighttime comes and you are ready to go to sleep, turn out the lights, turn off the radio, put out the cat, and lie down in bed, lie on your back. Put your feet close together (some people like to cross their ankles, but beware of the bones digging into each other) and clasp your hands together over your chest. Let them rest lightly on your chest as if you were praying. (And I suppose you are—praying to get some sleep!)

Then say to yourself, "Okay. I'm going to go down to my Alpha level, down to the color *lilac* (or *violet*), and when I get there I'm going to be *ready to fall asleep."*

Then close your eyes, and visualize the color *Red. See* it and keep thinking about it until you actually do *see* the color *Red* inside your head.

Then say to yourself, "I'm going *down* to the color *Orange."* *See* the color *Orange, see* it your mind's eye. Keep thinking about orange until you have it there, even if it's only for a second.

Then say to yourself, "I'm going *down* to the color *Yellow*."

*See* the color *Yellow*. *See* it come into your mind's eye and keep thinking about it until you are satisfied that it has appeared.

Then say to yourself, "I'm going *down* to the color *Green*."

*See* the color *Green*. Keep thinking about it and trying to bring it in until you are satisfied that you have seen green inside your mind.

Then say to yourself: "I'm going *down* to the color *Blue*."

The same thing. *See* the color *Blue*. Make it come into your mind's eye and keep it there until you are satisfied that you've seen it.

Then say to yourself: "I'm going *down* to the *last* color, the color *Violet*. When I see *Violet* I shall fall asleep."

Then bring the color *Violet* (or *Lilac*) into your mind's eye. Keep it there until you are satisfied that you have seen it.

Pleasant dreams!

Most insomniacs will fall asleep *before* they get to the final color. One student in El Paso, Texas, came to me the day after she had tried the exercise, complaining that she would get to green and then have to wake herself up and stay awake until the violet level was reached.

Is this self-hypnosis? I suppose so, but it's also conditioning. You are setting up a system whereby your Sub-Conscious will know you want to fall asleep. Once you've done this a few times, you can just lie there, take a quick glimpse of red, and zoom right to the bottom color.

If you get to the bottom color and you are still awake and *aware* that you are awake (think about that one for a minute), then tell yourself, "I'm in my Alpha level. I will be going to sleep any minute now"—but it's only on rare occasions that that will be necessary.

A woman in Cleveland, Ohio, gets down to her final color and then sees her entire body enveloped in a fine lilac mist. She just floats off with it and awakens the next morning.

Should you go to sleep normally and waken during the night, don't get angry with yourself (always keep your emotions at low ebb when you wish to sleep) and don't take a sleeping pill. Just get back into the position (on your back, ankles together or crossed, hands clasped over your chest) and start seeing the colors again, all the way down to the *violet or lilac* level.

Do you want to take a quick nap in the afternoon and be refreshed for an evening away from home? Lie on the bed and go down those colors.

Tired and need a few minutes just to relax? Lie down and say, "I'm only going to relax. I don't want to go to sleep. I just need to relax and regroup my energies." Then start the color countdown. Ten minutes' rest like this is worth several hours of sleep at night.

Are you in a situation in which you're becoming nervous and tense? Are you biting your inner lip in anticipation of whatever is coming? Close your eyes (you can sit up for this one) and visualize the colors. Just go down the colors and by the time you get to the bottom level, you'll be calm, cool, and collected.

Naturally, something this easy and beneficial isn't going to be relegated to the back of your psychic medicine cabinet, to be used only when you're suffering from insomnia. We'll use this exercise several times in the experiments to follow. Like the Cosmic Forces, it has many many uses and so you should master it as soon as you possibly can.

# LESSON 6

# Your Secret Place

## YOUR SECRET PLACE

When I was a child I had a secret place in the woods about a mile behind our home in Ohio. I carved it out from under the bushes, flattened out a cardboard box for a floor, and put in a couple of my favorite books. At one time I even thought about bringing in electricity so someday I could have my own moving pictures. It was my favorite place because it was mine *only*, the one spot in the entire world that belonged to me, and nobody else could get in unless I invited them.

As I grew older (and wiser!), I realized the need we all have for a secret place where we can get off by ourselves and not be disturbed. (The secret place of one lady in Phoenix, Arizona, is her bathroom. She goes in and closes the door and stretches out in the dry tub. She says it's the only room in the house where her family doesn't bother her.)

There is a psychic secret place that you can go to—a place that is exclusively yours, where you can relax, dream, and store up energy for your return trip back into the real world.

I will not presume to tell you where it is, or what it is. It is so secret that even you won't know about it until you reach it. Then, there it will be, fully developed, spread out, and inviting only you to enter. Once you've found it, you can return whenever you wish, knowing it will be there and knowing you will have it all to yourself. It's easy for you to reach but impossible for anyone else to desecrate. And "desecrate" is the right word, for your place can become as sacred as a chapel, as impressive as a church, as inspiring as a cathedral.

If you're ready, come with me. I can take you to the *door* of this place, but I cannot enter.

If you've been playing the radio or the television, turn off these outside noises. The best place to begin a visit to your secret place is in the quiet of your own bedroom. If this is impossible, then tell others living with you that you're going into another room and don't wish to be disturbed. If they ask what you plan on doing, tell them quite simply: to take a trip.

Sit in a comfortable chair. Put your hands loosely in your lap and keep your feet flat on the floor.

Take a deep breath, hold it, exhale slowly. Do it again. This time when you are breathing in, *see* the White Light of protection coming into your nostrils and filling your lungs. Breathe in and feel the calmness of the White Light as it enters your body and begins to spread itself throughout your system. Just sit there, breathing comfortably, *feeling* the White Light coming in and working within you.

Now visualize the color *Red*. *See* it in your mind's eye. Actually *see* it and know that you have seen it, even though your physical eyes are closed.

Now go *down* to the color *Orange*. *See* it. Know you have seen it.

Now *down* to the color *Yellow*. *See* it. Know you have seen it.

Now *down* to the color *Green*. *See* it. Know you have seen it.

Now *down* to the color *Blue*. *See* the color *Blue*. Know you have seen it in your mind's eye.

Now *down* to the *final* color, the *last* color of the chart, the color *Violet* or *Lilac*. *See* it, experience it. *Know* you have it captured in your mind's eye.

Now see yourself standing surrounded by the color *Violet* or *Lilac*. Actually *see* your physical body standing as if in a mist or a cloud of the color violet or lilac. Don't try to rush it. Let it come gradually, but don't do anything else until your physical body has been covered in this soft, conducive, and highly spiritual color.

When you have reached this violet, alpha level, then, *with your eyes still closed*, look in front of you and you will see that you are standing at the end of a corridor. The corridor is made completely of white marble. The walls are marble, the floor is marble, the ceiling is marble. It is not a very long corridor. There is a light at the end of this corridor. Start walking down the corridor in the direction of the light.

When you get to the light, stop.

Now in front of you, if you'll look down at your feet, you'll see that you are standing at the top of a staircase. There are steps in front of you leading *downward*. What the staircase is made of is not important to me, but maybe it is to you. Put a staircase there that suits your own personality and thoughts—a staircase that you would like to have in some private mansion inside your soul.

There are 21 steps on this staircase, and in a minute you are going to start down them, going all the way down to the bottom. You will wait until I tell you to descend.

As you go down the steps *I want you to see yourself descend-*

*ing* the stairs. I want you to see your physical body going down the stairs. *See* yourself. *Feel* yourself descending the stairs as they are counted under you.

All right. You are on the top step. The 21st step.

I want you to step down to the 20th step.

Down to the 19th step.

Down to the 18th step.

Down to the 17th step.

You are getting deep into your Alpha level.

Now to the 16th.

To the 15th.

14 . . .

13 . . .

12 . . .

11 . . .

10 . . .

You are getting deeper and deeper.

On the 9th step.

The 8th.

7 . . .

6 . . .

5 . . .

You are almost there.

4 . . .

3 . . .

2 . . .

1 . . .

You are at the bottom of the stairs. Both feet are on the landing at the bottom of the stairs. You are deep into your Alpha level. You are deeper into your own self than you have ever been before.

Yet: You are in complete control of yourself at all times. You can, just by opening your eyes, return back up to the normal conscious level. There is no danger. You are where you are because you want to be there. Not even loud noises like cars or telephones will disturb you.

Take a deep breath and feel the rarefied atmosphere of this new level.

There is a door in front of you. Look at it. Describe it. Examine it carefully. What kind of material is it made of? Wood? Metal? Steel? Glass? Is it painted, studded, natural color? Any designs on it? Does it look light or heavy? This is *your* door, your door to your own secret place. Look at it carefully so you will recognize it the next time you see it.

Now look at the lock and handle. What are they made of? What color are they? Are they light-looking or heavy-looking?

There is a key in the lock. Take the key out of the lock and examine it. What kind of material is it made of? What color is it? What style is it: modern, baroque, Gothic?

Now put the key back in the lock. Turn the key. Open the lock. Before you open the door, know that behind it is a scene from nature. *It is your Secret Place.* Expect to see an outdoor scene. Expect to see *your* particular private scene.

Now open the door.

Step inside.

What do you see?

Take your time. Look around you. Walk into your scene and look all around you.

Are there trees? Mountains? Birds? Flowers? A river? Clouds in the sky? Rocks? Green grass? *What do you see?*

Look around. If there is something there that you don't like, *change it.* This is your private world, so you can change it to suit yourself. If there are mountains and you don't like mountains, *just erase them* and they will *disappear.* Change what you don't like.

Are there things missing? Would you like a running stream? Then put one in there, wherever you choose. Just by wanting to have something, you can have it. This is *your* Secret Place. You can do with it as you choose.

Listen for sounds. Are there any? Birds? Music? The sound of the wind rustling the leaves? *Listen* to the sounds of your Secret Place.

Take a deep breath. Bring in the air of this new place. What do you smell? Flowers? Perfume? Freshly mown grass? Take a deep breath and bring into your lungs the freshness and purity of this incredible air.

Now continue your wanderings in this place. Walk around and look and approve, or change. Find a comfortable place and sit down, maybe under a tree or maybe at the edge of your brook. Maybe you want to perch on a rock, or maybe you just want to stretch out on the grass and stare at the blue sky.

Go ahead. Do whatever you wish, letting the beauty and the

purity and the peacefulness of the place saturate your very being.

I'll be quiet for about ten minutes. This is your world. I have no right to intrude. . . .


Okay! Sorry, but time is up. I hate to take you away, but you can always come back. You *will* be back several times before the course is over. It's time to go.

Get up from where you have been sitting or lying, and stretch. Look around you. Make sure the things you wanted in there a few minutes ago are still there. Make sure the things you removed are still gone.

Now walk back toward the door. When you get to the door, turn around and take a deep breath. Take one more deep breath of this magnificent atmosphere. Now turn around and go out the door. Pull it shut after you. Turn the key in the lock. Make sure that the door to your Secret Place is locked. Put the key in your pocket.

Now turn around and you'll see that you're facing that staircase. Stand at the bottom of it, and as I count, see yourself stepping on each step and going *up* the staircase to the top of the stairs.

Ready?

You are on the 1st step. Now move *upward* to the 2nd step.

Now up to the 3rd.

Up to the 4th.

Up to the 5th.

You are going back *up* the stairs now.

To the 6th.

To the 7th.

To the 8th.

The 9th.

The 10th.

You are halfway to the top.

Up to the 11th.

The 12th.

13 . . .

14 . . .

15 . . .

Higher and higher now.

16 . . .
17 . . .
18 . . .
19 . . .
20 . . .
21. You are on the top step.

Now turn back the way you first came and you will see the marble corridor. There is a light at the other end of the corridor. Start walking toward that light. When you reach it, stop.

Now let yourself be bathed in that violet or lilac color. Feel it all around you like a mist or a fine cloud. *See* yourself surrounded by this *Violet* or *Lilac* color.

Now that color changes *up* into *Blue*.

It changes *up* into *Green*.

*Up* into *Yellow*.

*Up* into *Orange*.

*Up* into *Red*.

Welcome back to the surface of the earth! Open your eyes. You've taken a successful trip.

Now that you know where your Secret Place is, you can return to it whenever you choose. When you need a few minutes' relaxation, go down those stairs and in through that door. When you need to have the answers to certain problems, go to your Secret Place, get comfortable, and put the questions out into the rarefied air down there. Then sit, calmly and relaxed, and *listen* for the replies that will *surely* come to you.

Your Secret Place is an invaluable piece of real estate (it is certainly very "real" for you), and the more you visit it and call upon its regenerative powers, the more real and substantial a place it will become and the better it will serve you.

A student in one of my classes was also enrolled at U.C.L.A. Before an exam, he would get so uptight that he would forget everything he had studied. Even the Little Man wasn't able to break the stone wall he had constructed for himself between his Conscious and Sub-Conscious storehouse of information. So, just before he would enter the classroom for an exam, he would find a quiet spot on the campus lawn and spend a few minutes in his Secret Place. "It left me calm, rested, and sure of myself as never before," he told me. "I get energized but it's a different kind. It's not that frantic thing that others get when they 'turn on' to something they hope will help them. I also

67

*know* that I have all the answers to any question I might be asked. I let the information flow through me and onto my exam paper. It's great!"

A well-known television actress who took the class in Los Angeles uses her Secret Place whenever she has to do a stage play. "Doing a T.V. show is one thing," she says, "but the stage is different. You can't have retakes and editing. You're out there naked in front of a lot of live people, and you have only one chance to do it and it must be done right. Before the curtain goes up, I take a few minutes in my dressing room. I tell everyone not to bother me and I head straight for my Secret Place. It has lots of open fields and flowers, but it also has a golden fountain with the sweetest, most sparkling water I've ever seen anywhere. I don't know who installed that fountain for me—it was there the first time you sent me to the place. I take a crystal goblet that is always sitting on the rim of the fountain and fill it with that water. Then I drink it. It calms me, it gives me courage, and it turns me into an actress; not just the old T.V. face everyone knows. The fact that I have a Secret Place is one of the most important discoveries of my adult life. Too bad I didn't know about it when I was a child."

Okay. You deserve a break after that trip, so get up, walk around, have a cup of coffee, and stretch.

# LESSON 7

# Contacting Anyone in the World

The Sub-Conscious mind, as I've said several times, is one of the most amazing mechanisms ever invented. And just think: You don't have to go out and buy one especially for this course—you've already got one, which is a considerable savings right there!

You've all heard the stories of mothers who "felt" that their children were in danger and rushed home to find they'd been correct. I knew a young couple who'd recently had a child; about three months later, they went out to a dinner party for the first time since the child had been born. At the party the mother suddenly turned to her husband. Her face was ashen and she was trembling. "Something's happened to the baby!" she said.

"Nonsense," he replied. "The baby-sitter has this telephone number. If anything was the matter, she'd call."

But the young mother was so insistent that they left the dinner table and drove quickly home. They rushed into the house and found the baby-sitter in the living room watching television. They dashed into the bedroom. The baby was in his bed, but somehow he had managed to get a wool blanket wrapped around his face and was slowly smothering to death!

Now, how did the mother get the psychic message to come home?

If you would like to turn back and look at Figure 3, Lesson 2 again, you'll see more clearly what I'm talking about in this section.

The child, *even though it was unable to speak,* sensed its danger. He knew that he needed help. In his young life there was only one person who was always there to help him: his mother. So he began to cry out on a *mental level* for his mother. The cry was carried into his Sub-Conscious and the Little Man, seeing that there was no way he could contact the mother for the baby, put out an urgent telephone message to the Super-Conscious: "Find the baby's mother!"

The Super-Conscious *easily* traveled the thin new connection between the child and the mother and dashed the message into her Conscious Mind with such force that it upset her physically. She got the message, listened (!), and hurried home, thereby saving her child's life.

Another case, quite sad but also quite common in times of war: A soldier in Vietnam is suddenly hit by a bullet. He clutches at his stomach, and as he falls to the ground he thinks, "My God, I'll never see my mother again!" and dies.

Back in the States the soldier's mother awakens from a sound sleep. "Good Lord," she says to her husband, "something's happened to Johnny!" The telegram that arrives a few days later proves that she was absolutely right.

What was the process? Johnny, knowing that he was hit and probably knowing he was going to die, sent one last frantic message to his mother. His Sub-Conscious flashed it to his Super-Conscious connection and it was almost instantly transmitted to his mother's Super-Conscious, down to her Sub-Conscious, and into her Conscious Mind with such force that it woke her up.

Several years ago, after I had left Brazil and was living in San Francisco, I began to hear the voice of a most wonderful little woman whom I often called "my Brazilian mother." She did not have my California address and while I couldn't make out what she was saying, I knew that she was trying to tell me something. Immediately I sent her a telegram (like most Brazilians she had no phone) and a few days later a letter arrived. Yes, she had been very anxious to contact me and to tell me of a rather sad event that had taken place in "our" family. She had gone into a church and prayed that I would somehow get in touch with her. We were both gratified—but not surprised—that the message service had worked.

Cases like this are not new or unique. They happen all the time. Quite probably you yourself have had such messages delivered from your Super-Conscious.

We all have someone we feel especially "close" to. There must be a member of your family, a friend, a lover—someone with whom you have strong psychic connection. Each of you usually knowing what the other is going to say before it is said; if the other is in trouble; ill, or if you are thinking of each other. There is "something" that seems to connect you with this particular person, "something" that comes in so strongly that you've often picked up the phone, dialed his or her number, and asked, "Is everything all right?" The first couple of times this happened, you and your friend probably laughed about it and were amazed that it "worked." But now that it has happened several times, *you are used to it.* You take it for granted. You even practice it. Fine—that's the way it should be. What we are going to learn now is how to use this same Sub-Conscious to Super-Conscious telephone connection to phone *anyone anywhere*—and, usually, get an answer.

I want you to *know* that you can do these things, and I want you to keep at them until they become natural, everyday occurrences. Once you've reached that stage, then information and ideas will flow freely. And while the element of surprise will be gone, there will be a warm feeling of accomplishment and the sensation of never being alone.

I hope these examples and the drawing in Figure 3 have made clear to you how and why this contacting operates. Now let's go to *work*.

In order to contact someone by means of this Super-Conscious telephone, you must have known that person and have set up a sympathetic relationship between you. The ancient Hawaiians believed that each time you shook someone's hand, a fine thin strand of thread was created between the two of you, and no matter where you went or how long you were gone, that thread still existed and could be used to make a mental contact.

Those of you who wish to contact Liza Minnelli or Paul Newman, forget it. If you haven't met them, your plug isn't in.

The strongest connection seems to be between mother and child. Possibly this is because the child was created from the mother's very flesh and blood. I don't know, and so far science hasn't tried to examine that aspect of family relationships. (And it will be a cold day in Acapulco when the average scientist gets around to even admitting there might be such a connection! A friend of mine often says, "The superstitions of today will be the sciences of tomorrow." I hope so, for the sake of everyone coming after us.)

I want you to think about someone you know rather well and who knows how to locate you—in other words, has your address or your telephone number or knows a third party who does. This should be someone you haven't seen in a little while.

Now sit in your chair with your feet uncrossed on the floor and your hands resting in your lap. Close your eyes.

Let's say, for purposes of illustration, that your name is Mary Ann Jones and you want to contact Howard Smith. The fact that you don't know where Howard Smith is doesn't matter; the fact that he knows where *you* are does. Got that?

Now picture Howard Smith's face in your mind's eye. Just as you brought in the red and the blue and all those colors, now bring in Howard's face. *As you are doing this,* say to yourself: "Howard Smith, this is Mary Ann Jones. Please contact me! Howard Smith, this is Mary Ann Jones! I want to talk to you! Contact me! Howard Smith, this is Mary Ann Jones calling you!"

The words don't have to be exact, but you get the idea. You are sending out a forceful message to Howard Smith that he *will* receive via his Super-Conscious.

If Howard is one of those clods who never listen to their astral messages, you might have to keep sending the S.O.S. for several days. The fact that *you* know what is happening at your end doesn't necessarily mean that Howard is aware of it at his.

Repeat this message as many times as you like over the next few days. Unlike the request to your Little Man to dig up a long-forgotten fact, which mustn't be repeated too often after the first command, you can keep badgering Howard's Super-Conscious as much as you like. When your Little Man sees it's still the same outgoing message, and he has nothing to do with it once it's sent, he will just leave in the cosmic telephone plug and you'll have an open line to Howard's Super-Conscious.

Depending on the force of your desire to make the contact and on the force of its reception in Howard's Conscious Mind, you'll probably get a letter or a phone call from him. *Why* he is calling you he won't be able to say, but he'll probably start off with, "I was thinking about you and wondered how you were doing."

Sometimes Howard will make contact through a mutual friend rather than do it directly. The friend will call you and say, "Howard was here for dinner last night and all he did was talk about you. Why don't you phone him?"

I recall a lady in Georgia who had taken this course and never tried to use any of the techniques until it was almost too late. She had a daughter, an only child, who had run off during the 1960s to become a hippie. The daughter had never called her mother after she left home, and the woman had no idea where in the world her child was—or even *if* she still was.

One day the mother suffered a massive heart attack. She managed to get to a phone and call an ambulance. The next day, in the hospital, she overheard two nurses discussing her case. There seemed to be no hope for a recovery. She was going to die.

The only thing the mother really wanted before she died was to talk to her daughter again. Recalling the link between their Super-Conscious minds, she sent out the message: "Ruthie, this is your mother. Wherever you are please call me."

She sent it over and over and over again.

In a bar in San Francisco, Ruthie suddenly sat bolt upright and said to her companion, "Something's the matter with Mother. I've got to call her."

She went to a pay phone and called her home in Atlanta. There was no answer. Then Ruthie called a neighbor and said that she was trying to contact her mother. The neighbor told her that her mother had been taken to Atlanta General Hospital. Ruthie phoned there, the switchboard operator pushed the right key, and in less than four hours after she had started sending the message, the lady heard her daughter's voice from the phone beside her bed.

I hate to get emotional, but this true story does have a happy ending. Ruthie was so pleased to find her mother still loved her that she flew back to Atlanta and moved back into the family house. The mother, now with a reason to go on living, recovered in double-fast time, left the hospital, and is still alive and well and happy with her rediscovered daughter. It's at times like those that I say, "Thank you, spirits!"

# LESSON 8

# Selling Whatever You Have to Sell— Especially Yourself

We've all heard of the salesman who could sell iceboxes to Eskimos. The salesman's lot is a difficult one, with more put-downs than positive responses from the people he meets in any one day. It isn't easy to be a salesman; you need a strong constitution and an even stronger ego.

Yet each one of us is a salesman. We are all selling *ourselves*.

Now don't pull back in righteous indignation and tell me you're not selling yourself, because you are. There is not one person alive who isn't trying to convince the world that whatever he has is worth paying for—and I don't care if that person is an Avon lady trying to convince a housewife to buy her wares and become instantly beautiful, or the housewife later trying to convince her husband that she is worth all the money he (indirectly) shelled out for them.

People sell themselves all the time. Movie stars do it when they make a film and hope people buy tickets. Authors do it when they write a book and hope it becomes a best-seller. A soldier does it in hopes of becoming a general. A businessman does it for promotion or to impress another firm. A schoolgirl does it when she worries about her hair being combed. Even the family cat does it when he comes back with a mouse in his mouth to show you he's really been out there taking care of the place.

Whatever we have in the material world, we have because we have sold ourselves in one way or another to get it. If you doubt this, just look at your own life. What have you accomplished and how much of it was done completely on your own? Where would you be today if someone hadn't been convinced (that is, "sold") that you could do the job? See what I mean? We are all salesmen (or sales*persons,* in deference to women's lib) and we survive in this society by selling ourselves to others. Make no mistake about it.

Then if this is true (and it is!) the job of selling should be refined to the $n$th degree. Unfortunately, most of us fail to sell ourselves because we don't know the proper techniques. I'm not writing a book for insurance salesmen or shoe peddlers, but both of those professions could profit from the psychic formula you're going to learn next.

You have already seen how you can bring in the Cosmic Forces or outside energies to have them do anything you want them to do, especially in giving you facts and information. You've already seen how you can contact anyone anywhere in the world to get your message across. Now let's look at how you can convince someone that what you have for sale is what he wants to buy.

Once again, this thing you have for sale does not necessarily have to be a product. It can be an idea or project, or you may be trying to convince this man to give you a job.

Let's say that you have applied for a job at the Astorbilt Corporation. You have met Mr. Astorbilt himself and he seemed to like you, but admitted that he had several other applicants for the one position that was open. He would make up his mind and call you in a few days. If you didn't hear from him . . .

After the interview you go home and you begin to think about that job. You really do want it. You would be good at it and you would be good for the company. Yes, you decide you want that job. Mr. Astorbilt just has to choose you! So what do you do about it?

Stand with your feet slightly apart and your arms down at your sides and do the Cosmic Forces formula. Three times the Forces are brought in. On the fourth time *thank them* (!) for everything they have done for you in the past and tell them about the new job possibility. Tell them about Mr. Astorbilt and tell them how great you'd be for that company if only they would give you a chance.

Then picture Mr. Astorbilt sitting behind his desk. That's what Figure 4 is all about. Picture him sitting there in the office where you had the interview, and then stretch out your right arm. Stretch it out and point your index finger. You point your finger and *in your mind's eye you are touching the forehead of Mr. Astorbilt.* You are reaching out and touching Mr. Astorbilt on the forehead! Actually *see* him, actually *touch* him!

Then take a deep breath, filling your body even fuller with the Cosmic Forces, and send those Forces down your right arm and out your right index finger *into* Mr. Astorbilt's forehead. Send the force with all your mental strength. *See* that energy running *down* your arm and *out* your finger and *into* him. Actually see it and feel it. Know that you are touching this man's forehead and know that you are influencing his thoughts.

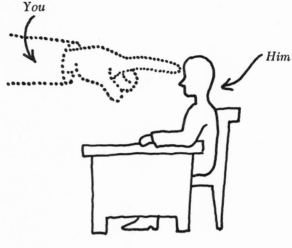

*Figure 4.*

Then say: "Mr. Astorbilt, this is John Smith." (Use your own name. You don't want some stranger named John Smith getting that job!) "I want that job you talked about to me. I want that job! I would be good for the company and the job would be good for me. I can do it! I can do it better than anyone else you will see for that job! Mr. Astorbilt, this is [your name] give me that job! I want that job!"

Keep sending this thought and this energy, *all the while picturing your finger touching Mr. Astorbilt's forehead.* That's very important. Never lose mental sight of Mr. Astorbilt. Then you will "feel" that you have sent enough. There will be something inside you (a little voice?) that will say, "Okay, that's enough." Then stop. Go about your own business and don't bother with Mr. Astorbilt until the next morning. Then zap him again. Zap him several times during the day, and zap him with all the energy you can work up.

If you have done it correctly, there are nine chances out of ten that Mr. Astorbilt will call you either to ask you to come for another interview or to offer you the job.

Let's look and see what you've done.

You have deliberately set about to contact Mr. Astorbilt's Super-Conscious. You have zapped him through your Little Man, and by sending all that energy your Little Man has kept the lines open between your Super-Conscious and Mr. Astorbilt's. As you did when you tried to contact a distant friend, you have told the Little Man to keep the message circuit open. He's done that and you have a clear line straight into Mr. Astorbilt.

Let me tell you a true story of how I once used this technique.

A friend of mine in Hollywood is a rather well-known actor—at least he is today. At one time he was completely unknown and Hollywood couldn't have cared less.

He heard through the grapevine that a certain television producer was casting a soap opera. He had read the script a few months before and knew that there was a part in it that he would be perfect for. But each time he wanted to try out for the part, the producer was always "too busy," "in conference," "out to lunch," "out of town." The time for the show to begin rehearsals was drawing near and, in desperation, my friend came to me.

Would I please do some of my "spooky stuff" and get him the part? Or at least get him in to see the producer so he could convince him that he was right for the show? I told him I would *try*. (Never *promise* miracles—they're always blowing up in your face.)

I told my friend to go to the great man's office the next afternoon at 2 o'clock. When he protested that he didn't have an appointment, I assured him it didn't matter. Then I asked for the full name of the producer and his address. Could he describe the producer's office? No, because he had never got that far, but he did describe what the reception area looked like. That was enough.

At two the next afternoon the young man walked into the reception room of the producer's office. At the same time I started my "spooky stuff." I brought in the Cosmic Forces, I stretched out my arm, and I zapped that producer with enough energy to electrocute an elephant. I kept calling the man's name, telling him that this young actor was in his office and deserved to have a part in his soap opera.

About two hours later, this friend was at my apartment door with an iced bottle of champagne (French, of course!) under his arm. He had gone to the office exactly at two. When he asked the receptionist if he could see Mr. Big Shot, he was told that the man was very busy and nobody could see him without an appointment. So my friend hung around the reception area looking at the signed photos of movie stars. After a few minutes the great man came out of his office and walked over to the receptionist's desk. He asked the girl something, and when she replied he looked up and saw my friend standing there. "Are you an actor?" the producer asked him.

"Yes I am," came the reply.

"Come into my office," Mr. Big Shot said. "I'd like to talk to you."

The outcome was that after almost an hour and a half of readings and conversation, my friend *got* the part.

Coincidence? I don't think so. What force made the Great Man leave his inner sanctum and go out to speak personally to the receptionist? He had an inner-office phone; he could just as easily have talked to her over it, but he didn't. He *came out* of his office and *into* the *vibrations* of this young man, and he *noticed* the young man, and he was sufficiently impressed to take him back into his office. The producer was happy that he had found the right actor for the part. My friend was happy that he was going to work again. And as for me, the champagne was delicious!

At this point, there are some ethical considerations that must be examined.

First of all, don't expect to get that job if you're really not qualified for it. If you have a job changing the paper in the men's room, don't expect to get the job of bank president when it falls available. Don't think you can hoodwink the Cosmic Forces into giving you the president's position when they know you can barely handle the janitor's. They know what your capabilities are and, since they are constantly on your side—constantly looking after your best interests—they are not about to put you into a spot you won't be able to handle. They are not going to louse up everything they have worked for all of your life, just because you childishly think you want something else. They know what you *really* want, what you can safely handle. So don't get upset when you don't get the job that you *know* you couldn't manage if you did get it.

Because you do *know* what you can or cannot do. You may

not say it aloud in so many words, but you *know* when you are asking for the impossible. When you step too far out of line, you will get a physical sensation. "They" will give it to you. It's usually a sinking feeling or a twisting feeling in your stomach, telling you, "Come off it, brother. You know that's wrong to want."

An illustration: Your neighbor has a pear tree with some of the most succulent pears you've ever seen. But your neighbor is also an old grouch who won't give you, or anybody else, any of those pears. Then one day you see him get into his car and drive away. Knowing he is gone, you get a basket, cross over the fence into his yard, and head straight for that forbidden pear tree.

There is a "scrrrrrricik" sound in your stomach. Your stomach turns over a little. It's a message from your Little Man and from "them": "That pear tree is a no-no. Stay away!"

We all get these feelings when we are about to do something wrong. Thank goodness, most of us listen to the message and desist from the act.

So, when you are asking for the Cosmic Forces to give you that special job, pay attention to your stomach. If it does all sorts of acrobatics, then forget it. The job isn't for you and "they" are not about to work at getting it for you.

Now back to the specifics of this technique. The pointing-finger method works very well when you know who you want to zap. But let's say you want to make an impression and you haven't met the person to be impressed. A large company has placed an advertisement in the paper for an employee, and you want to apply for the job.

The first thing to do is phone the employment office of this concern and ask about the job. Stay on the phone as long as you are able and, if possible, get the man who will be doing the hiring on the other end of the phone. That could be enough physical contact to make the psychic contact later. If that can't be done (Mr. Importants rarely lower themselves to take unasked-for phone calls), at least find out the man's name.

Then, if the first screening is by letter only, write that letter (drawing on the Cosmic Forces to help you draft a *great* letter of application). When it's written, hold it in your *two hands,* bring in the Cosmic Forces, then see the energies pouring down your arms, out into your hands, and then into the sheet of paper you've just written. Zap that letter with all the strength you can muster. Really pour yourself into that sheet of paper. Then *without* delay, put it in the mail. If you've done it correctly, your letter will trigger something in the mind of the person at the other end, and you'll get an appointment to come in for a personal interview.

Now, supposing you are to meet someone that you've never met before and have to sell him something. This could happen if you're a door-to-door salesman or if you suddenly find yourself in a position you can't get out of: "Oh, do you want to see our chief buyer? You're in luck. Here he is now!" and boom—there you are face to face with the man, having had no time to work your energies on him beforehand.

Don't despair. And *don't talk.* Sit across from his desk (as straight across from him as you can) and let him do all the talking. While he is going on about the company and what the company needs and how marvelous the company is, you are sitting there drawing in the Cosmic Forces silently, and zapping him with streams of White Light. You've (I hope) been doing the Cosmic Forces exercise and you can now bring in the protective white light in just a few seconds. So you sit there, smiling at him and nodding your head, apparently interested in every pearl that falls from his lips—but giving him the double whammy with your own brand of White Light.

You do this by knowing your body is filled with this protective energy and then by sending it out of your body through your eyes. Pretend your eyes are two laser beams of White Light and you are covering this man with it, drowning him in it, putting him on the same wavelength as you are.

After a while he'll shut up and start to listen to you. He will be most sympathetic to what you have to say and what you have to offer. Even if his company doesn't really need another of whatever you are selling, he will probably buy one from you just because he likes you. He may not know *why* he likes you . . . but we won't let him in on the secret.

You will find that if you give the other person enough time to become covered with the White Light, you can bring him or her around to your way of thinking almost every time. Don't protest. Don't argue. Don't hard-sell. Just drown them in your own wavelength. I don't care what you are selling—they will be more interested in buying.

One again, it stands to reason that if this technique can be used for positive purposes—to get a job, sell a product—it can also be used for negative purposes. That is not the intention of this course, but I would be most foolish to tell you that what works in one way doesn't work in the other. I don't believe there is any good or bad—*only energy* and *how* it is *directed.*

We had a perfect example of this a few years ago in the United States. While Watergate was boiling up and over, a great many people fell out of love with President Nixon. The man had been elected by the biggest majority in the history of free elections; and then, to find him so implicated in such a seamy operation turned the millions who trusted him against him. They began to talk badly of him, became angry at him, began hating him. And they sent that hate to him. From all across the nation, great waves of hate engulfed that man in the Oval Office. So powerful was this combined hate-energy that very soon after his resignation he almost died.

There is a power and you can use it. Never doubt it.

# LESSON 9

# ESP Right Now!

One of the delights of this course is that you don't have to sit contemplating your navel for ten years or eat brown rice with no salt for three years to develop your psychic abilities. If I keep harping on the fact that we *all* have these abilities and that they are normal and everyone can develop them, please bear with me. I must repeat the message until you're tired of hearing it and you've begun to take it for granted. That's my job. Your job is to dig into yourself and bring these abilities to the surface.

It's always pleasing to me and surprising to the beginning students of my classes when, after the first day or two, they are seeing their own ESP work for them. The expressions on their faces are a delight, and frankly I get as big a kick out of it as they do.

I don't really like the term ESP. The E stands for "extra," as if psychic sensory perception *was* something extra. It's not. It's normal. It's part of your physical and mental makeup as Homo sapiens and there is nothing extra-ordinary about it. We have to have catchy labels for everything today, so obviously I can't get rid of the term ESP completely, but how about modifying it to MSP? *Mind* Sensory Perception. That's a better title and comes closer to the real source of this perception better than "extra" does.

Okay, let's get to *work*.

If you are reading this book with several others (which I heartily recommend), I want you to pair off. Find another person, and he or she will be your partner for this series of experiments.

Should you be reading this tome by yourself, now is the time to call in a few friends and ask them if they want to test their MSP. You'll be amazed at how everyone wants to try it. Your friends don't have to believe any of this *but* they must have an open mind on the subject. Don't ever try to do any of the experiments, in the beginning, with scoffers or mental deadheads. Don't waste your energy.

Bring in the Cosmic Forces. Get that feeling (which you should be aware of by now) running into your body. If you have to do this with persons who know nothing about the Cosmic Forces, just tell them to stand with their eyes shut and breathing deeply, imagining they have an automobile battery in their chests and the air they bring into their lungs is recharging it.

The important thing now is that *you* feel the power of the Cosmic Forces.

Find two chairs and place them facing each other. You sit in one and your partner in the other. Knees and feet should not be touching.

Reach out and clasp your partner's hands. Hold them lightly.

Now close your eyes and, as you did when you sent that energy down your arm and out your finger to the man at his office desk, send the energy down your arm and out your hands into the hands of your partner.

Now—in your mind's eye—see this energy flowing up through his arms, up into his head, coming out the top of his head, and returning back into yours. In other words, like so:

*Figure 5.*

Of course, as you are sending your energy to your partner, he is also sending you his energy, so that you really have a double flow going back and forth, up and around.

Also, of course, what you are doing is creating that silver thread that the Hawaiians believe remains between two people once they have met. By consciously creating this kind of energy link, you are creating the cables and wires that will be used to send your "MSP" messages.

Now, still holding hands, I want you to decide between you who is going to be Number 1 and who will be Number 2. There is no pecking system implied here; you simply have to decide who will go first and who will go second. Everybody has a turn, so don't be disappointed at being Number 2. Avis Car Rental has been Number 2 for years and is making a fortune from it!

Now, with the two of you still holding hands, I want Number 1 to think of a *color*. Think of a color and pass it over to Number 2 by means of that electrical wiring apparatus we have just strung up between you. Take the thought of the color and send it down your arms, out your hands, and into the hands and arms of Number 2.

As soon as Number 2 gets the message, he should say the *first* color that pops into his mind. Remember, Number 2, you are *a radio set* and are *receiving information* from Number 1, who is a *transmitter. As a radio set you do not have the right to analyze or reject the information that flows through you.* Your only duty is to listen for the information (in this case, the name of the color) and broadcast it immediately.

*Listen.* In the majority of times the *first* color that pops into your mind will be the correct one. Listen for it. Don't put yourself in the middle. Don't think, as so many students do, "Well, I know he likes red and is wearing a red shirt, so I bet the color he's going to give me will be red." *You stay out of it.* I cannot repeat this too often. Keep your own personality and thought patterns *out* of things psychic. You are only a *receiver* of impressions! A good medium is exactly what the word implies: a channel. The clearer the T.V. channel, the better the reception. Keep your channels clear of your own thoughts, personality, and preconceived notions. Got that?

When Number 2 has correctly told you the color, then mentally change places. Number 1 will become the receiver and Number 2 (I'm sorry I hollered at you a minute ago!) will become the transmitter. Number 2 will send a *color* and Number 1 must pick it up correctly.

Send these colors back and forth three times. Please stick to the basic colors. In one class in Chicago, an interior decorator insisted on sending her partner (a cab driver!) such colors as puce, chartreuse, and tawny!

Now let's try a new suggestion. Number 1 will send Number 2 a common masculine first name: Bob, Bill, John, or the like.

Again, please, no names like Chauncey, Ezekial, or Wilber-force! This will be a little more difficult, so don't become distraught, Number 2, when you don't get it the first time. Consider that you are on the right track if you get short names like Joe or Ed or Sam and Number 1 is sending a short name like Tom. But if you get long names like Algernon, William, and Matthew and he is sending Tom, you are off base com-pletely.

Send a masculine name to Number 1 now.

Okay, let's switch subject matter. Now send a well-known feminine first name, and let's rule Mary out right from the start. People always either send Mary or think they are going to get Mary. It's the commonest—and most confusing name in this type of experiment.

The same rules apply for the girls' names as did for the boys'. If you've been sending a long name like Elizabeth and your partner keeps getting things like Ann, Sue, and Fay, either you're not doing a good job of sending or he is doing a *lousy* job of receiving. *But* if you should be sending Elizabeth and he gets Betty, then consider it a job well done. Tom for Thomas, Bill for William, and Tony for Anthony are all counted as direct hits.

Let's do the same thing with names of states. Number 1 will send something like Maine and Number 2 should pick it up. (Remember, your hands are still clasped and you are still using that energy wire you've been building up.) Often senders will see in their minds the map of the state, including some sur-rounding areas, and send that, with the result that the receiver will then get the correct geographical area and then stumble around trying to pick out the exact state you have in mind. Of course, most states are surrounded by other states and it is this larger overall area that is frequently transmitted. *But* if you are sending Texas and your partner keeps getting Michigan, Ohio, and Kentucky, he scores no points. Do the states exercise back and forth for three complete sets—that is, six states between you.

By this time it should be becoming easier to send your thought messages. In the few, rare cases in which neither of you gets anything from the other, *Change partners.* For some reason, the connection has not been made and probably will not be made without a great deal of mental effort on both parts.

There is nothing sinful about changing partners at this stage of the game. I'd much rather have you try with someone else and see how this thing works than have you sit there determined that you can do it no matter how long it takes.

Now let's do the same thing with countries in Europe! The same rules apply about short names and long names and geographical areas, but I've found that few Americans really have a clear picture of what the map of Europe looks like. One boy in Ohio was sending Austria, and his partner (a college graduate!) wasn't coming up with anything. Finally she said "Germany," and he replied excitedly, "You're close!" She smiled. "Oh, if I'm close, it must be Egypt!" Wrong.

If you want to take a break for a few minutes, go ahead. But please refrain from coffee or cigarettes. You don't want to get your nervous system all doped up just when you've got it to the point at which it is starting to obey your mental commands.

Now let's get back together. This time the odds on one side of the room and the evens on the others. In other words, all the Number 1's on one side of the room and the Number 2's on the other. Form a line, facing your partner on the opposite side. Keep a good deal of carpet space between the two sides.

I want the evens to have pads of notepaper and ball-point pens—not pencils. A pencil tends to break under pressure, and you don't want anything to stop the flow once it gets going.

The odds will also have pen and paper in their hands, but relaxed and down at their sides.

The odds will now *turn their backs* on the evens.

Each even member will decide to *himself* on a symbol and will concentrate on sending that symbol to his partner on the opposite side of the room. By *symbol* I mean an internationally accepted design that your partner would know. For instance:

The even will decide on the symbol he is going to send, will say "Now," meaning that he is starting to send it (if there is a group doing this, one person will say "now" for them all), and he will begin to *draw* that symbol over and over and over again on the paper in his hand. He will trace it, going over the lines and at the same time sending that form to his partner via the psychic chord that has been established between them. If the even partner has chosen the infinity sign, for instance, his paper would look like this after a few minutes:

When the odd partner senses the figure she is being sent, she will draw it on her own piece of paper. Then she will turn around and face her opposite number. When *all* the persons on the odd side have drawn what they have picked up from the even side and have turned around, you can start comparing notes. Did you get what your partner sent? Did you get a circle and he was sending the symbol for infinity? If so, then you were picking up on his design. Did you get a triangle and he was sending a star? Again, count that as a direct hit. Did you get a triangle when he was sending a square? Also enough of a direct hit: he was sending four straight lines and you picked up three straight lines.

But if he was sending a star and you picked up three wavy lines, you missed. If he sent a dollar sign and you got a square, that's also a miss.

As you compare notes, you'll discover a common but unexplained psychic phenomenon. Quite often someone else will pick up the sign that was beamed in your direction. Your partner may have been sending you a star and you got a circle, but the person next to you got a star while his partner was sending a fish. It happens with greater frequency than not and, obviously, means that somehow your messages have been transmitted on the wrong wavelengths.

"Oh, come on," you'll say, "the law of averages make it certain that someone will be sending a common symbol and someone else will pick it up just because there aren't that many different symbols around!"

I might have agreed with you before the time I held a class in Mexico City in which a Mexican man sent his partner—another male Mexican—the Aztec symbol of a snake with feathers on its back. The only person to pick up that symbol and draw it exactly was an American girl who had just arrived in Mexico and had never studied anything at all about Mexican history or mythology. "I just kept getting this creepy snake with something funny growing out of it," she said. "I tried to chase it away but it came coming back. So I drew it."

Now have the odds do the sending and the evens try to pick up on it. The same rules apply.

When you have compared notes on this, I want the evens to go *out* of the room. Go down the hall, into another room, or even outside in the street or onto a patio. The evens will then get together and decide upon *one* symbol that *all* of them will send at the same time.

When this has been decided, the odds are notified that they can start to pick up now, and the evens, still out of the room, will start sending. Each member of the even side will draw the same symbol on his or her paper. If you have eight evens, then you'll have eight similar drawings going on at the same time.

Now the odds must get together and decide on one symbol among them. They must come to *one* conclusion. They must all agree on *one* particular design being sent. When they have agreed, someone tells the evens to stop sending, and to come back into the room. The odds then show what they were picking up and the evens show what they were sending. This experiment can be a little more difficult because of the space that is now between the two groups and the stretching of the psychic chords. But if it is practiced enough times, it can be done with greater and greater accuracy.

Once symbols have paled, I like to have one group send the name of a well-known movie star. The only stipulation is that the other side know in advance if it is a male or female personality. Once again, please refrain from using Marilyn Monroe and John Wayne. It seems those are the two first chosen by everyone. If "Mary Is A Grand Old Name," then so are John and Marilyn!

The advantage of working with a partner is that you can continue these experiments after the class is over. They can be done at any time or under any conditions. If you create a strong rapport with your partner, the two of you can be sending each other messages all the time.

MSP is like playing the piano: The more you practice, the better at it you will become. You don't need any real talent to play a lively "Chopsticks" and you already have the talent inside you for real MSP.

# LESSON 10
# Psychom-
# etry

That fancy ten-dollar word means holding something in your hand and getting the vibrations from it—no more than that.

After a while, all objects take on the personality of their owner, and just as fingerprints cling to a drinking glass, your psychic print remains on things you wear and touch. Don't ask me why, because I don't know. This phenomenon, like so many others in this field, has yet to be investigated scientifically.

Quite often a good medium will be able to give you a reading just by holding an object belonging to you. Again, like the radio set, she tunes out the world around her—especially her own thoughts—and tunes in to what the object is transmitting. Then she reports what is coming through to her. If she is right, you should tell her so and she'll know she has tuned in to your particular vibrations. Then the reading will continue with ease and (one hopes) with accuracy.

In Los Angeles there is one well-known medium, the Baroness Lotta von Strahl, who has helped the Los Angeles police solve innumerable cases by the exclusive use of psychometry.

One of her most famous cases was that of the Manson killings. The day after they found the bodies of Sharon Tate and her friends in all that blood and gore, the police came (secretly, of course!) knocking at Lotta's door. They had objects that belonged to the victims and also a knife or two that they were sure must have been dropped by the killers. What could she see?

Lotta took the objects and began to have horrible pains. She felt the stabbings in her back and stomach and, a few times, was tempted to ask the police to go away and not force her to go through this torment. But she kept on. She said that she picked up the name "Mason" or "Maxon," and that the man was small, with piercing dark eyes. She also said that the killers were not just men but that there were women with them, and young girls at that. She was puzzled when she kept getting "the same last name. You know," she told the officers, "it's almost as if they were all members of the same *family*." Then she saw something that puzzled her. It was an old town in the days of the Wild West but "nobody lives there. It's strange, but the doors are open and the houses have no substance."

Of course, when Charles Manson was finally caught, he did have several girls with him who formed his "family." They had been living at a ranch that served as a location for shooting Western films. What Lotta had seen was the empty false fronts of the movie set.

Another case involved a violent murder at a Mexican-American wedding. The groom had been stabbed and the bride was wounded. The police had arrested several suspects, but none of them admitted committing the crime. The police gave Lotta the dead man's shirt, all torn and brown with dried blood, and she picked up something about a man with a birthmark on his upper-right shoulder. The police had photographs of the corpse. No, he didn't have such a mark. "Then," said the medium, "the murderer has such a mark. If you find the man with this birthmark, he will confess."

The police called in all the suspects and asked them to remove their shirts. One had a birthmark just where Lotta had said it would be. He denied killing the bridegroom, but when the police told him about Lotta and what she had seen, he began to scream about witchcraft, broke down, and confessed.

Psychometry is easy, especially if you practice and if you— what's the magic word?—*listen.*

Here it is terribly important to *listen* to the information you get from the object. Don't hesitate to say something because *you* don't feel it applies. *You must stay out of it.* It is vitally important for your success that you keep *yourself* out of it as much as possible. Once again, you are only the radio receiving the message—and radios don't think or decide what they will broadcast.

The first time I ever tried psychometry, I was interviewing two wonderful mediums in San Jose, California: Marcia Warzek and Norma Dart, for my book *The Psychic World of California.* Both women had been doing psychometry for a large audience that afternoon, going from row to row and telling people things about themselves no stranger could possibly have known. The audience was amazed and, I'll confess, I was impressed. Later that evening I said to Norma, "That must be very difficult to do, isn't it?"

"Not at all," she said, and promptly took off her bracelet and handed it to me. "Just relax, close your eyes, and tell me the first thing that comes to your mind. Don't force it and don't try to analyze it. Just let the images come and I'll tell you if you're right or not."

I took that bracelet (a little self-consciously, for after all, they were the psychics, not I!) and as I held it, I started to smile. "What's so funny?" Norma asked.

"I've got a dumb picture here," I said with some embarrassment. "It couldn't possibly mean anything, because it doesn't have anything to do with you."

"Well, what it is? You let me decide if it's for me or not."

"I see a large sailing ship," I said, "with its sails unfurled, and it's going across choppy water." I opened my eyes and handed her the bracelet. "See? That meant nothing at all."

"Oh no?" Norma got up and went out of the room. In a few minutes she was back with a book in her hand. "When my husband died recently, I decided to take all his books and incorporate them into my own library. I wanted to have the same bookplate in them that I had in my own books. I've been combing San Jose for the past month trying to find that bookplate. Look!" She opened her book and pointed to the bookplate. It was a picture of a ship, its sails unfurled, going against a rough sea.

After that, I did psychometry for my family and acquaintances, even saved a friend of mine a few dollars on the purchase of an antique Chinese vase. She was anxious to have it, but the dealer wanted $500 for it. She took me with her to help make up her mind. I know quite a bit about American and English antiques but nothing about Oriental art. Yet as I picked up the vase I decided to do some psychometry on it. The first words I got were "not old."

"Should I buy it?" she asked me, with the dealer standing right there.

"No," I said with great authority, "It's not old. It's a fake."

The dealer looked thunderstruck. "What do you know about the Ming period?" he asked haughtily.

"A great deal," I lied, "and this vase is not more than thirty years old and not worth more than fifty dollars."

He was sure I was from the police and began to apologize for having tried to sell us something that wasn't genuine. We walked out in righteous indignation and had a good laugh about it in a nearby bar. My friend bought the drinks with some of the $500 I had saved her.

One of the first times I ever did psychometry in public was in Dallas, Texas. I was lecturing on various aspects of psychic phenomena and when I mentioned that it was possible to get information from inanimate objects, a lady in the front row got up and handed me a very expensive diamond wristwatch. "Let's see what you can get from that," she said.

I held the watch and looked at the lady. She was superbly dressed in the very latest fashion—Gucci shoes, diamond necklace, Louis Vuitton handbag, the works. There I stood before over four hundred people and what did I get? A tumbledown shack, an old Ford up on cinder blocks, and two or three small children running around with bare feet, dirty clothes, and ratted hair.

"Well?" she said.

I gulped, trying to get out of this public fiasco and wondering if Texans still used guns to run charlatans out of town. I decided to play it honest. "What I get can't have anything to do with you. There is a shack, an old Ford, and some dirty half-naked children playing around it."

"Oh yes," she beamed. "That does mean something to me. That was the way we lived until Daddy struck oil!"

I repeat: Keep *yourself* out of the reading!

The longer an object has been worn, the stronger the vibrations will be. When giving a reading, ask for something the person has carried with him for a while. A key ring bought just a few days ago won't tell you anything, but a pair of glasses worn for five years will be an encyclopedia of information.

Also make sure that the object has had only one owner. If someone gives you a ring that has also been worn by her mother or her sister, you may well get conflicting vibrations. Often I've been telling someone things and she'll say, "No, that doesn't mean a thing," and *then* she'll tell me that she bought that object in a secondhand store or antique shop. I have no way, then, of knowing *who* the vibrations belong to.

When you are giving a reading, insist that the person be entirely honest with you. If you say that he drives a green car, and he drives a brown car, tell him to say so. Many people will want to please you, and they will stretch the truth (or just plain lie) to "help" you along. They are only confusing things because until you start getting the truthful "Yes, that makes sense" answers, you have no idea whether you have tuned in to that person or not. Insist that people be honest with you, it'll help you give them a better reading.

Every now and then, you'll find yourself telling someone things, they'll go along and admit that you are absolutely right, and then you'll hit one item and they'll balk: "No. That isn't me. I don't know what you're talking about." If the image in question fades away and doesn't repeat itself in the reading, then most likely you were wrong. But if it *keeps* returning or won't go away, and the person keeps denying it, it is almost 100 percent certain that this person doesn't know or doesn't remember what he or she is talking about.

I've had people tell me, as much as a month later, that I had been correct and they just hadn't realized it then. I remember with one woman I kept getting the name Sarah. No, she didn't know any Sarah. The name came back and wouldn't go away. "I have the impression that this Sarah is in spirit and is guiding you, protecting you," I said. No, she had never had a Sarah in her life. I must be wrong.

Then, about three months later, I got a letter from the woman. She had gone back to visit her aged mother and had told her of the reading. When she mentioned the name Sarah, her mother almost fainted. The first child the mother had ever had was named Sarah, but she was born with a severe deformity and only lived a few days. The mother had never told any of the children that came after Sarah that they had had a sister who died.

The information may be given to you in many different ways. You may get names, dates, places, and so on—by "get" I mean you'll *hear* them inside your head or else you'll *see* them written out in your mind's eye.

You may get colors, or heat or cold. You may get symbols. You may see an eagle, for example, and know this person doesn't keep eagles as pets or shoot eagles on her days off, so the big bird must be symbolic of something. Don't try to interpret the eagle symbol *unless* the interpretation is given to you immediately after the image. If all you get is the bird, then give her the bird and let her interpret it to her own satisfaction.

One last thing that is *very important. Never* give someone a reading who doesn't want it! It will only end in disaster, with you looking like the main candidate for the Nobel Prize for Jerks. If someone says that he doesn't want to have anything psychometrized then *don't* insist. You will get no cooperation from this negative soul but will be blocked at every level by his negativity. Don't say I didn't warn you!

Any further questions, dear students? Good. Let's get to *work*. Find yourself someone (the less well you know them, the better) who has an object and wants a reading. Have that person take off the object and hold it in her hands. Tell her to close her eyes and imagine currents of electricity running down both her arms into her palms. Have her recharge the object to put even more of herself into it. Then, when you feel ready to begin, ask her to hand it to you.

Say whatever comes into your head. You may start to get words or names even before the object touches your own hands. Fine—say what you get. Keep asking for confirmation of your facts. Make the person say yes or no or maybe, but get her confirmation in some way or else you won't know if you're on the right track.

If you don't get anything at all, ask for another object and hold *both* those objects together. You can pass the objects from one hand to another if you choose, press them against your forehead, do anything with them (within reason!) to make you closer and more in touch with their vibrations.

If you still don't get anything, pass the objects back. Either ask for another item to hold or forget the whole thing with that particular person. And remember, just because you bomb out with one person doesn't mean you'll do it with another. Maybe you just couldn't find that first person's wave length.

Keep at it until you get it right . . . and you will.

Okay, you may say, this is all very nice but what *good* is it? Why bother to learn this spooky stuff with the long name?

Good question! I've already cited two of the reasons: to help track down a murderer and to decide if something, like the fake antique vase, is really worth the price.

But there are other reasons. You are about to sign a contract, say. You hold it for a few minutes and "something" just doesn't feel right to you. You ask to take it home and study it overnight. Then, in the calmness of your own study, you read the small print at the bottom! No way do you agree with those terms!

You get a letter from a friend. He is saying one thing but by holding his letter and "listening," you get what he was *thinking* as he was writing—and that was something completely different. I'm not suggesting that you'll get his exact words, but you'll get his mood and his emotions, and you'll be able to judge for yourself whether or not to take his letter at face value.

On being introduced to someone, you reach out and take his hand. Blaaahhh! comes back the response in quick psychometric fashion. Uh-huh, you say to yourself, I'd better *watch* this fellow.

I've had students who were collectors of various and sundry things use their psychometry to cut through all the muddle at flea markets and head straight for the items they would be interested in. It saves a lot of time and shoe leather.

I myself like to collect occult and psychic books, especially those written before 1940. I've gotten so that I can go directly to such books in the most jumbled shop and my hand will reach for the interesting ones first. Furthermore, if the book has been signed by the author, I *know* the signature is in there before I open the cover.

There are many ways psychometry can be used in your daily life. After all, that's why you are taking this course, correct?

# LESSON 11

# Seeing the Aura

The aura is the field of energy that runs around the human body, or emanates from it, or encircles it, or covers it—nobody has come to any agreement as to exactly what it is or what it does. Theories abound, of course, but then in this business, everyone is entitled to a theory. Why not? They're free.

The Brazilian spiritists (who are very big on theories) have decided that the aura is a magnetic field of energy that runs clockwise around every human body. It is *a part* of the body, yet also *apart* from the body. The Brazilians think this energy is part of the mind force and, like it, comes from an outside source at birth and vanishes at death.

Some photographers have actually taken pictures of "something" leaving the body precisely at the moment of death. British author Guy Lyon Playfair in his excellent book *The Indefinite Boundary* tells of a French doctor named Hippolyte Baraduc ". . . who took several pictures of his wife immediately after her death. His prints show what look like large lumps of cotton wool floating above her corpse. He also took a picture of his teen-age son, who died in 1907, after he had been placed in a coffin. Again, the print shows clouds of misty something-or-other almost blotting out the body. Baraduc was thought to be an honest man, though he failed to convince the world he had photographed spirit bodies."

Author Playfair adds a note of his own: "I cannot imagine what kind of man would deliberately fake such experiments with members of his own family." Playfair also tells of pictures of the aura or spirit body and relates with some relish the "gruesome experiment in which a French photographer cut the hand off a corpse and found that by heating it to body temperature he got results on film similar to those obtained from a living person's hand."

Shall we call it "soul" or "psi-body" as Playfair does, or *prana* as the Yogis do? At this stage of psychic research, you pays your money and you takes your choice.

I want to call it "body energy," if I may, and I am firmly convinced that it functions as a result of the Little Man back there in the Sub-Conscious.

When you are ill, the *color* of this body energy changes. Alberto Aguas, the amazing Brazilian psychic healer now working almost exclusively in the United States, has been able to describe the colors that he sees around a person and then see how they have changed once he has put new energy into the client's aura. He has worked with many doctors and is able to tell where a person is physically ill just by the "black spots" he sees around them. He claims that the energy field around a healthy body varies from clear white to golden. When a person is not feeling well, that clearness turns cloudy, almost gray. He says that illnesses show up first in the aura and then are transferred to the flesh and blood. "By learning to see the aura," he says, "we can often detect an ailment days before it actually shows up in the body. If everyone learned to do this, especially doctors and nurses, we could replace the black spots in the aura and eliminate physical pain and discomfort."

We'll get into this in more detail in the section on healing. Right now let's look at a few auras, or body energies.

It's always better to start out with your own energy field so that you know what to look for in others. The majority of my students have been able to see their own energies, but a *few* haven't. If you are one of the few, don't despair.

It's also better to do this with three or more people because often when you can't seem to find your own energy field, you can see your neighbor's, and that will help you recognize yours when you do see it.

It's very simple.

Turn the lights down *low* in the room or pull the drapes if it's daytime.

Find a wall or a large piece of plain furniture like a kitchen cupboard or a console radio and T.V. set that has a *light, clear* surface. Stay away from a wall that is dancing with patterns. Stay away from furniture that is dark or stenciled with designs. The idea is to find a flat, clear, lightly painted surface.

Turn your back to the light. You are now facing your own shadow.

Put your hands in front of you, at about belt level, with the palms facing you. Place the finger-tips of one hand against the finger-tips of the other. Keep the fingers open so there is a space horizontally between them. Like this:

*Figure 6.*

See that wavy line between the fingers, the one I drew running up and down? I want you to stare at that line, especially where the fingers are touching one another.

Now, slowly, that's s——l——o——w——l——y, move your hands apart in a horizontal movement. As you do this, keep staring at the place where the wavy line is.

Do you see the *white* lines of energy that seem to *stretch* as you pull your fingers apart?

Do you see the masses of energy that are in between your open fingers?

How about the energy that seems to be up and over your thumbs?

Keep trying until you do see this. It will help if you can see your neighbor's energy.

If you don't have good results, possibly you aren't holding your hands at the proper angle. Maybe you are in too *much* shadow, or maybe you are really not looking in the right places.

It is difficult to explain this process through words in a book. In the classes it's hard enough in the beginning, but then one student will give a shout and see his energy. Others will look to see what he is so happy about and then find their own and start to help the others who, for some reason, just can't make it.

A lady in Mexico City couldn't see her energy if her life depended on it, yet everyone else saw it quite clearly. She even made zig-zags in the air and we could all see the patterns her hands left. She never did see it and was furious with all of us.

As to seeing the entire body energy of others (not just what is emanating around the hands), some people claim that it helps to look at a person out of the corner of your eye. In other words, turn your head away and look at him as if you didn't want him to know you were watching him. This has never worked for me, but it has for a few folks I know, so it's worth a try.

We have gotten excellent results by turning down the lights, having one person stand in front of a solid-colored wall (white, cream, or tan are the best background surfaces), and then staring at him. When he starts to move, you can see the energy moving with him. At times it's necessary to look at him from an angle rather than straight on. Get up and move around until you see that "something" that seems to be surrounding him. (Many people have seen my energy field when I've been lecturing on stage. A combination of the background curtains, the overhead lights, and the fact that I'm moving while they are sitting still enables them to see this physical-yet-psychic phenomenon.)

Once a lady in the audience at Akron, Ohio, asked me if I saw auras. At that time, I had never given the subject much thought, or really tried. "No," I replied, "I don't think I ever have."

Then suddenly, like an effect in a Hollywood film, I saw a blue haze of sparkling energy all around her. "But I see one now!" I shouted in amazement. "I see yours!"

I met a young man in San Francisco who had seen these energies all his life and had taken them for granted. It wasn't until he was in his early teens that he learned everybody didn't see them. His mother told me that when he was a child and they would visit a friend unexpectedly he would say, "She isn't home. I can't see her light coming under the door." And he was always right.

If you want to see this energy field, keep practicing on your hands and keep watching other people, especially as they move in front of clear backgrounds. Look around the head and neck and shoulder areas—it's usually stronger there.

# LESSON 12
# Healing

Whenever someone asks me what good all this psychic knowledge really is, I always mention healing. I will continue to mention it because I've seen so much of it and I've seen it work. It is not something invented by hysterical antimedicine types or terminal cases seeking a miracle. Healing works. It has worked for thousands of years in all cultures and in all faiths. It is still working today, even though the majority of people tend to pooh-pooh anybody who says he can heal but doesn't have a medical degree to prove it.

The healing I am talking about has nothing to do with pills or injections or hospitals. It has to do with this *energy* we've been discussing right from the start, and with your mind-power abilities.

Entire books can be written on the subject (I wrote one called *Psychic Healers,* as a matter of fact) and I don't intend to go into all the ramifications here. What I do want to do is tell you how you can start using these healing energies.

We've already talked about the Little Man and his abilities. I've told you about saying "Oh no!" when you get some kind of an ache or pain and telling the Little Man to take it away. Once you have given him the order—given it to him strongly and with the proper wording—he'll carry out your instructions to the letter.

A few years ago I had to be in Cincinnati, Ohio, for a series of television and radio appearances about a new book of mine. I'd been in tropical places like Brazil and California for quite a while and so was not prepared either mentally or physically for the nine inches of snow that fell on the city the day I got there. The stuff seemed to be being dumped from boxcars, and soon everything was buried in it. The city was as unprepared as I was; they didn't have enough snowplows, enough trucks to haul it away.

That night when I phoned room service for dinner I was told that the snow had kept the night crew at home, with the result that there was no food in the hotel. You know how you want something even more when you are told you can't have it? Well, my desire to eat suddenly turned into a raging appetite. Figuring there must be something open someplace in the downtown area, I pulled a couple of sweaters on over a couple of shirts and dashed out into the blizzard. There was little movement, but the streetlights were on so I could see which drift I was heading for.

You know those metal doors they have in the sidewalks near large stores—the ones that open up to receive merchandise and then close again? Well, one of those contraptions was hidden beneath the snow and covered with ice. I came dashing across it, then suddenly felt myself being thrown into the air. I put out my hand to break the fall and when I hit the ground I landed on my hand, my hip, and my ankle. I am not exactly Twiggy in my physical build and when I come down, I come hard!

Even though I was in pain, I limped for another block or two and finally found a greasy spoon that was open. After some soup and coffee I limped back through the snow to my hotel. By the time I was ready for bed, my hand was bruised and swollen, my hip was blackening with small red veins to decorate it, and my ankle was throbbing and swollen. I got into bed, turned out the light, and pictured myself the next morning crawling out across the television studio stage to tell everyone of the remarkable curative powers of the mind. What a farce! Maybe I should call and cancel the whole thing?

Then the thought came to me (from the Super-Conscious?): "You idiot! Why don't you practice what you preach? Heal yourself!" So I got out of bed and I called in the Cosmic Forces. I sent them first to my hand and pictured a thousand tiny lightning bolts striking at the bruised part and cleaning away the debris. Then I sent the energy to my hip and pictured it being bombarded from all angles by those magic bolts of energy. Finally I aimed my thoughts at my ankle and zapped it with all the energy I could muster, telling the Little Man repeatedly that I wanted him to take away the pain and the bruised patches. Then I got back into bed and, miraculously, fell sound asleep.

In the morning I got up, took a shower, and got dressed. I was on my way out of the room when I suddenly remembered my bruises. I looked at my hand: fresh and clean. Then I took off my trousers and examined my hip: no bruise, and no raised blood vessels. Then I peeled off my sock and inspected my ankle: perfect condition. Happily I walked to the television station and almost danced across the floor. When I told of the "miracle overnight healing" I'd given myself, the smart-alec host didn't believe me—but that was all right because I knew a lot of people who were watching at home did believe me, and I was aiming for them, not him.

The next time you have a serious ache or pain (or one that could *become* serious if you worried enough about it) stand up, relax, call in the Cosmic Forces, and *visualize* them at work in that bothersome area of your body. Visualizing them helps to send the energies there, as if you were directing a flashlight beam in the dark.

You can visualize these working energies in any manner you choose. I like to see the lightning bolts stabbing away at the illness and leaving fresh, healthy tissue. Some people see arrows shooting into the area and destroying the blackness. A lady friend of mine in Reno, Nevada, sees a tiny little doctor and a tiny little nurse dressed all in white and standing beside a tiny operating table industriously cutting and swabbing. The method best for you will come to you as you try this.

Let's get into the healing of others.

The first rule is: *Don't try to heal someone who doesn't want to be healed.* As egotistical as that may sound, it's a basic truth of this metaphysical business. To be healed, people must *want* to be healed. They must give their Little Man the order that they are tired of their physical condition and want to be whole and well. *Asking* for a healing—whether the request be put to a member of the AMA or to you—is a conscious command to the Sub-Conscious that the person really wants to get better. If you come on too strong, trying to convince someone to let you help him, he may agree just to *please you,* while all the time he is thinking—and sending the message back to the Little Man— "This isn't going to work, this isn't going to do a damned thing." And of course it won't.

I have known many people in my travels who are always ill, and I expect you know a few too. They have a cold one day, a fever the next, a sore leg on Tuesday, and a pain in the rear on Friday. Headaches keep them from enjoying themselves, and their constant complaints keep people around them from enjoying themselves too. You feel guilty having a good time if someone with you is dying of terminal negativity.

I had a relative who was a terminal hypochondriac. There wasn't a day that she didn't have some new disease or some new complaint. In the morning we'd ask, "How do you feel?" and she'd say, "Oh, I had this terrible pain during the night and didn't sleep a wink. It started here [the leg], moved over here [the right shoulder] and now it's here [around the heart]." The pains always ended around the heart. When her friends would telephone and innocently ask, "How are you?" they too would get the adventures of the galloping pain. After a while the family stopped asking and the friends stopped telephoning. The lady had a miserable life brought on by her own negativity. The only way she could get any attention—she thought—was to have some sort of illness that nobody else had. She also, I should add, sent herself to the hospital many times with cases of real things like pneumonia and inflamed gall bladder—they were real because she so wanted them to be!

She devoted her lifetime to dying. Despite the dozens of doctors she consulted and the quantities of pills she took, she didn't get better because she *didn't want* **to** get better. No doctor could cure her, she bragged, and no medicine was ever strong enough to completely rid her of whatever she had at the moment.

She could have been blasted by the most powerful psychic healing forces in the world and they would not have had the slightest effect. Sending her healing energies would have been a waste of time and power—and both are too precious to waste.

How does someone ask you for help? There are many ways. First, of course, is the outright "Hey, I know you're into psychic healing. See what you can do with my back." Then there are the people who will say, "I have this pain. Do you know anything I can take for it?" Or your small child may climb on your lap and moan, "Mommy, I'm sick." That is the same thing as saying, "Heal me, Mommy."

If the problem is mental and the person is unable to ask for help, you know instinctively that inside he is silently shouting to be normal. You can send him healing. If a person is an alcoholic and tells you, in his remorseful sober moments, that he would love to give up the bottle, you may take that as a request to send him the energies. The same goes with someone addicted to drugs. Let me add right here that drugs interfere with all mental energy patterns, so don't be discouraged when your efforts seem to have little or no effect. The best time, by the way, to send your energies to alcoholics or addicts is when they are asleep—zap them when their Conscious Mind is not awake to resist.

## PERSONAL HEALING

If the person who has requested the healing is in the same house or apartment with you, then the energies can be felt almost immediately and results can be seen more quickly. Here's what you do:

First stand and bring in the Cosmic Forces three times. *Thank them* for all they have done for you in the past, and then tell them about the friend or relative who is with you and needs a healing.

Ask them for the healing energies. Ask them to fill your body with these energies and to make these energies flow through you. Stand there with your palms upward and sense the energies pouring into you. *See* the White Protective Light covering you and *feel* the tingling in your palms or in your spine that will tell you that you've been filled with the energies.

Then immediately go over to the person who is ill—let's say it's a child in bed in the next room. Go to her, stretch your hands out over the affected area (sore throat, bruise, cut, or such), *but do not touch her body*. With your palms about two inches away from her, close your eyes and send the energy that has been building up inside you *down your arms* and *out* through *your palms*. See that energy leaving you. Feel that energy going.

Don't be alarmed if your hands get red or even quite hot. That's normal. Move your hands from time to time in an up-and-down or back-and-forth manner around the child's body. If she is ill all over, allow your hands to hover and glide all around her. Send the energies to every part of her. What you are doing is recharging her electrical body force with your newer and stronger electricity. You are strengthening her "aura," giving her physical body new force with which to recuperate.

If you are working on an adult and the person has, let's say, a sore shoulder, then have that person sit in a chair with you standing beside him. Put one hand in front of his shoulder and the other hand behind it. You are creating a positive and negative current *through* his body. Don't be surprised if your hands seem to take on a life of their own and you feel yourself urged to run them along his spine, around his forehead, down his legs, and so forth. Don't fight these urgings, obey them. Quite often an illness may appear in one spot but actually have been caused by an imbalance in another area of the body; it might therefore be necessary to recharge the person's entire electrical body. Your hands will know what to do.

The reason for not touching the person's body with your hands is that you are not really sending energies into his *body*, but into the electrical current running *around* his body. You are trying to give new force to his body-power, not his physical flesh and blood. By placing your hands directly on the body, you would be passing through the electrical field. You don't want that—you want to stay inside the field. Got it?

As you are working, ask the patient what reactions he is feeling. Don't *tell* him what he will feel. Don't plant ideas in his head. Let him tell you. He will probably say that he feels "heat," "tingling," "cold," "numbness," and quite often, when it is over, "dizziness."

You will know when to stop. *Listen* and you will be told "That's enough," either in those words or others. The Brazilian healer Alberto Aguas knows that a patient has had enough energy when he feels the backs of his own hands getting hot: "Then I know the energy is coming back at me, that the client's body cannot take any more. That's when I stop."

Let the patient sit or lie there for a while after you've finished with him. He may be too dizzy to get up immediately and the peaceful feeling the energies have given him is usually so relaxing that he won't want to move for a few minutes. While he is relaxing, go into the bathroom or kitchen and *wash your hands under cold running water*. Always do this after you've worked on someone. This stops the energy flow and also cleans your hands of anything you might have picked up from the ailing person.

## HEALING ANIMALS

Animals are very easy to heal because they will come to you wanting to be healed. A dog will limp over and crave affection, a bird will flutter near you, and even the solitary cat will let you caress her when she's not feeling well.

Animals heal easier because they're smaller. A healer once

explained it to me as "filling a vessel with water. The smaller the vessel, the quicker it fills."

After one of the healing sessions in my class in South Africa a lady went home to find her canary on the floor of its cage. It had been ill for days; its feathers were moulting and it wasn't eating. She was sure that it was dying. She called in the Cosmic Forces, reached into the cage and picked the little bird up in her hand, then sent all her energies into it. In a few minutes she opened her fist. The bird hopped onto its perch and began to sing. She was delighted. Her doubting husband and children were flabbergasted.

About the only time you touch a body in healing is when it happens to be the body of an animal. They seem to need the physical contact and the reassurance that you are sending them love. Then, too, if you crouch down near a sick animal, waving your hands and wiggling your fingers at it, it is going to back quickly away from you, positive that you are sicker in the head than it is in the body. Cats especially don't like hands floating around them from all angles.

If you have a sick animal, *pick it up in your arms* after you have filled your body with the Cosmic healing forces. Hold it in the crook of one arm, with one hand on the left side of its body and your right hand on the other. Again, you are sending the current into its body in a polarization of positive and negative.

Naturally if you have a sick horse, I don't expect you to pick it up in your arms. Larger animals can be treated like humans, and in these cases it's better not to touch them. Let your energy flow first into their electrical rather than into their physical body.

## HEALING AT A DISTANCE

If the person who is ill is at a distance from you—and it makes no difference if he is on the other side of town or the other side of the world—the procedure is different.

First of all, bring in the Cosmic Forces and fill your body. Then *see* the ill person in his surroundings. If you know that he is in St. Joseph's Hospital, Room 715, in Warren, Ohio, picture a hospital; then picture a door with the number 715 on it; and then picture the person in the hospital bed. In other words, *focus* your energies in on him.

If you know he's at home, picture the house, the room where he might be, and so on. If you know nothing more about his surroundings than the name of the town he lives in, picture a map of the state, then see the name of the town on it, and then picture the person. If you don't actually know the patient but have been requested to send healing by a friend, then get as much information about him as you can; age, physical structure, and so on. Of course, you must also know from what ailment he is suffering.

Once you have him in your mind's eye—once you *see* him mentally— then *place your hands on your body at the part where he is affected.* If he has a heart condition, place your hands over your own heart. If his problem is blindness, place your hands over your own eyes. If it is a leg problem, then put your hands on your own legs.

Then say: "I am touching the heart [eyes, legs, whatever] of Mr. John Jones [or whatever his name is] and the energies are going into *his* body."

Send those energies into your body with the same force that you'd use to heal a sick child in the next room. *Focus* upon Mr. Jones and *aim* your energies into his body no matter how many miles away he is.

Then, once you've heard the inner voice tell you "That's enough," stop what you're doing, cross your arms over in the Egyptian double-cross fashion, say "Thank you, thank you, thank you," and go wash your hands.

If you make a note of the time you sent the healing and then get someone at the other end to verify what the person was feeling at that time or just a few minutes afterward, you'll be very pleased at the physical sensations that "unexplainably" came over him.

Alberto Aguas does a great deal of absent healing (as do all professional healers). He was having good results with an elderly woman in West Virginia as he sent her the energies from California. One day she phoned him and said, "Wait a half hour longer before you send the healing today." Naturally, he asked her why. "Well," she replied, "I've been thinking that since I live on the eastern side of the mountain, you have to send those energies through all that rock. Today I'm going to go around to the western side of the mountain so they'll be stronger when they get here!"

## HEALING GROUPS

I always like to see class groups continue long after I've left town, getting together to experiment on one another and to bolster faltering faiths with their recent psychic exploits. The one thing I especially like to hear about are the results of the groups' healing efforts.

In many cities these groups (and other groups too, of course, the ones from my classes don't have the monopoly!) meet once a week in someone's home. Their procedure is as follows:

The members all stand in a circle, holding hands, and bring in the Cosmic Forces. Then they ask that the energy start to move around the circle. Each member mentally sends it to the person on his right, who sends it to the person on her right, and so on. By the time it gets back to the leader of the group, the energy is going rapidly around the circle. We have seen the temperature of the room rise several degrees, mouths become dry, and some of the participants staggering with the force that swirled through them. You can do the same and you can have the same results.

If there is someone in the group who needs a healing, that person unclasps his hands from the others and steps into the center of the circle. The gap left in the circle is quickly filled in by those on each side of him reaching out and clasping hands.

The individual to be healed tells the group what is the matter and *points to the area on his body* that he feels needs the healing. That way all the members know where to focus their energies.

The leader of the group then asks everyone to stare at that place on the person's body and to *send the healing energies like laser beams from their eyes;* to stare at the affected area and to send out the energies as they stare; to focus that force into powerful beams of love and understanding.

The bigger the group, of course, the more energy can be worked up. I have seen people in the center of the circle suddenly begin to perspire, shake, turn beet-red or ashen, stumble and—on one memorable occasion—pass out completely.

We had an ongoing group in Los Angeles for a while in which there was a young man (only twenty years old!) with three malignant brain tumors. The doctors had opened him up, said there was nothing to be done, sewed his scalp back together, and given him three months to live. He heard of our group and came to us during his supposed last month. When he stepped into the center of the circle, the force was so great that he clutched his head and passed out. The next time he got into the circle he staggered and finally had to sit down. After a month of these "treatments," he went back to his doctor. The man couldn't believe it. The tumors had shrunk to about one-tenth their size and seemed to be inactive. In March of 1975 the young man had been given three months to live. As of this writing, he is still alive and healthier than ever.

Once the healing group has taken care of those who are present, then each person is asked to name someone who is absent but needs healing. One by one, the names are said and each person *imagines* his or her ailing friend standing in the center of the circle. Then the leader asks that all the members stare into the circle *seeing* their particular friend in there— *seeing* their friend being bombarded by these energies; *seeing* their friend whole and well again. It's always fun to come to the group the following week and relate the tales of what the absent friends suddenly felt at the exact time they were being healed. Even better, of course, are the stories of how friends no longer need to be put into the circle because they have been healed.

At a healing circle in El Paso, Texas, we put in the name of a young man who had been in an automobile accident that very morning and was about to be operated upon. The doctors were sure that he would lose a leg. Before we did anything else, we began that circle by pouring love and energy into the patient. The next day we got the report: The doctors couldn't understand why the leg was so much healthier than it had appeared in the x-ray! The damage had become almost minimal. The leg was saved.

Psychic healing has been examined by some scientists in recent years and its physiological effects on the body have been corroborated. *The Psychic News* of London recently published a short article, "Healing Changes Blood Cells," that I'd like to quote:

> A professor of nurse education at New York University said she has evidence that laying-on-of-hands helps the sick by altering the hemoglobin levels in red blood cells.
> Dr. Dolores Kreiger devised a pilot scheme to test her theory. A group of 32 nurses and 64 patients were divided

into two sections. Hemoglobin is responsible for transporting oxygen from the lungs to the tissues.

The first group of patients received "healing" twice; the second group had routine nursing care.

In the 32 treated patients, "We found a significant change in the hemoglobin levels," said Dr. Krieger. "The 32 given only routine nursing care showed no significant changes in their hemoglobin levels.

"Nurses should become more aware that their contact with a patient at the bedside does have an effect upon his well-being."

A prominent Phoenix, Arizona, family physician, Dr. William McGarey, said the change "is not psychological. It's the real thing. Purposeful touch by hand with the intent to heal definitely can have a helpful effect on a patient."

Dr. Erik Peper, professor of interdisciplinary sciences at San Francisco State University said the hemoglobin level alteration "is hard proof that some physical changes take place as a result of healing. It raises one's resistance to illness and improves health."

Don't get me wrong. I'm not saying that psychic healing is the answer to *every* ailment or that we don't need doctors and their medicines. Often these healings just don't work, and nobody can explain why. Even with the most ardent "believer," a healing may not come about. These energies probably have their own rules and patterns they must follow to function properly. What these rules and patterns are, nobody knows. I only know that healings often *do* work and they *will* work for you with astonishing frequency when you apply them. Psychic healing has been around too long, in too many cultures, over too many centuries for anyone to doubt its reality. Christians, of all people, should believe in this type of healing if they believe at all in the Man who founded their religion. Remember the woman who only touched the hem of His garment and was healed?

# LESSON 13
# The Pentagram

I am always amazed at people who think that only the current, the present-day, has value, and that everything discovered years ago has no validity at all. They seem to have the idea that anything that's old can't be of any value in the present. If you look at the occult book market, for example, you'll find that there are hundreds of excellent books on the used-book shelves that nobody reads because the information is "old." Yet let some new writer come along, steal and simply rewrite what is in those books, and everyone rushes out to buy the book because it's "new."

There is no "new" knowledge in the psychic area.

It has all been known before, many times, by many other peoples. It has been around longer than any of us can remember, and it will be here long after we ourselves have gone into spirit.

If you haven't understood this, you haven't understood the very nature of what you're trying to accomplish. You aren't reading a course on plastics, rock music, or jet motor mechanics. You're reading about man's mind, what powers it, and the powers it contains. You are studying about things that go farther back than the alchemists, farther back than the Egyptians, farther back than the men in skins who scratched animal drawings on the walls of their caves. You are studying about the inherent nature of man himself—the basic powers God gave to Adam and Eve . . . and that we have been denying ever since.

Go out, then, and read the great psychic books written years—sometimes centuries—ago. Your psychic education shouldn't stop with this book. Use it as a stepping-stone to lead you back to ancient concepts such as that of the pentagram.

Several hundred years ago a psychic/religious doctrine that had been handed down in Judaism for generations was put onto paper. It was called the Cabala, and it was a guide, at times deliberately confusing in its explanations, to the development and use of psychic powers. That the ancient Jews knew about these powers and used them is obvious from the Old Testament that later grew out of the Cabala. It is full of psychic happenings: the Burning Bush, the Tablets on the Mountaintop, the parting of the Red Sea. Some say that the Ark of Covenant was in reality an "electrical battery" that amplified the powers between man and the spirit world. Even the belts of precious stones that the rabbis wore were designed to use the "power" of the various gemstones encrusted on them.

One of the many ritualistic symbols used by the ancient Jews was the pentagram. *They used it because it worked.* They've been using it for centuries, and it keeps on working. Many of my students have used it and I can tell you it has worked for them.

Let me give you an example. I was lecturing on the pentagram in Los Angeles when a student showed up with a friend of hers. Normally, I don't like outsiders coming into a class, but this was a postclass get-together and informal. (Not that my classes are *formal!*) The friend was having problems. She was being forced to move from her apartment because the building was being torn down for a freeway. (I predict that in 50 years there will be no more buildings in Los Angeles—just freeways.) She had to get out of that place in four days and was desperately looking for another apartment. When I started demonstrating the pentagram, she asked if her problem could be worked out on it. I said, "Why not?" However, when I told her that she could have anything she wanted—how it came and how much it cost wasn't important—she decided that she didn't want to move into another apartment. She wanted to live in a beach house in Malibu, and she only had $165 a month to spend for rent.

Well, you can hardly rent garage space in Malibu for $165, but it was her pentagram and she had the right to ask for anything she wanted. I said, "Let's go."

She went home that night and did the pentagram with a vengeance. The next day she drove into Malibu and started looking. She came upon a lovely small house on the beach. She stopped and asked the white-haired lady coming out the front door if she knew of any houses in the area for rent. After all, *I* had told her she would find one!

The lady said that there was one a few doors down, but the owner wanted $750 a month for it. As they talked, the lady discovered that the girl had gone to the same college back East that her daughter had attended. The girl said that she had known of the woman's daughter, but had only met her a few times because she was so popular and always surrounded by so many other friends.

Then the lady began to cry. Did the girl know that her

daughter was dead? She had died of cancer several months ago, and this was her daughter's beach house? The mother lived in the Midwest and had come to Malibu to pack her daughter's belongings and sell the house.

"You wouldn't consider renting it, would you?" the girl asked timidly.

The mother beamed. "To someone who knew my daughter and would respect her memory, yes I would. She loved this house and I think she would rather have it lived in by someone she knew than by a stranger."

"How much do you want for it?" the girl asked.

The older woman looked at her. "I don't need the money myself," she said, but if you would make the monthly mortgage payments to the bank, you could have it for that amount."

The amount? You guessed it—$165 a month!

*A pentagram will work only for material things.*

Don't try to use it to improve your health, get a new husband, or zap your enemies off the planet. It won't work. It must *only* be used when you want a material wish fulfilled. And, as you will see, it has to be *desired* with all your heart . . . not just wished for.

Let me show you how to go about it.

First, what do you want? You must know exactly *what* you want and exactly *when* you want it and exactly *where* you want it.

Remember, it is not your concern *how* you get it. The delivery technique is up to "them" upstairs. But you must give them the exact information with all the loose ends tied up neatly. If not, they will deliver it sloppily and haphazardly— that is, as you requested it.

Let's look at a typical—and American—sentence.

*"I want a new car."*

All wrong! Maybe you do want a new car, but that sure isn't the way to go about asking for it. Now you must take that sentence and enlarge upon it, yet at the same time refine it and *define* it.

What kind of a new car? "A Cadillac."

What color? "Blue."

So, redo the sentence: *"I want a new blue Cadillac."*

Better, but still all wrong.

Do you want this year's model, or can it be a 1959 model but in new condition? "Oh, this year's!"

Of course, in the automobile industry "this year's" model is actually last year's, since they've already started selling next year's. "Right. I want the latest model."

Can it be a new car but be full of defects? "Oh, no. I want it to be in perfect running condition."

Redo the sentence: *"I want a blue Cadillac, latest model, and in perfect condition."*

Okay, but there are still some loopholes. When do you want this car? Next year? In ten years? "I want it tomorrow."

Impossible. Never give "them" such a short working deadline for two reasons: 1) They've got to translate your emotions into matter and 2) You have to charge yourself up to the point at which you're ready to send the request. That may take hours, or it may take days, depending on you, your energy, and how much you really want this object. (Just a few years ago, an eminent and highly respectable California physicist came up with a theory and drew a graph as to how much energy was needed to make something become a reality and how long it took. I kid you not.)

"Okay. I understand. I want this car by the end of the year."

What year? *"This* year, of course!"

Okay, redo the sentence: *"I want a blue Cadillac, latest model and in perfect condition, by the end of this year."*

So far so good, but there are still a couple of loopholes that must be closed up before you start. *Where* do you want this car? Delivered to you in Detroit? In Plains? In Hong Kong? "Don't be silly. I want the car delivered to my home here in town."

Okay. Redo the sentence. *"I want a blue Cadillac, latest model and in perfect condition, delivered to my home by the end of this year."*

Satisfied? "Oh yes. It looks perfect."

But it's still wrong! "Wrong?"

Yes. You have the car delivered to your home. But where's the proof that it's yours and not meant for your neighbor? Shouldn't the papers be in your name? "Oh, God, that's right! I don't want anyone else to have this car. I'd better put that in the sentence!"

Good idea. *"I want a blue Cadillac, latest model and in*

*perfect condition, delivered to my home, the ownership papers in my name, by the end of this year."*

Fine, you've closed all the loopholes. Quite a change from the simple "I want a new car," isn't it?

Now comes the fun part.

I want you to take that sentence and break it down into *symbols*—symbols that only you will understand. In other words, if you are asking for, say, $10,000, you can't use the dollar sign because if someone else saw your pentagram they would understand what you were asking for. See what I'm saying? You can't use a symbol on your pentagram that anyone else can decipher correctly. As we go along breaking down this sentence, you'll see what I mean.

Let's start with "I," the first word of the sentence. What symbol would you like to use for it? "Well, how about my initials?"

No good. You can't use letters or numbers. You can't use anything that someone else might decipher. Got that? "I guess so." Well, how about a circle with a dot in it. That looks a little like an eye. Eye in place of I. See what I mean?

Okay, now having written out the sentence on a piece of paper, you draw the first symbol over the first letter. "I" becomes ⊙

The word "want" is scratched out. Of course you *want* this car or you wouldn't be asking for it.

The next word is "blue." "How about a capital letter B, but backwards?" Okay, "Blue" becomes ꓭ

Now you must find a symbol for "Cadillac." "How about a wheel with lots of speed behind it, like the cartoonists use?" Okay, so "Cadillac" becomes ○₌

"Latest model" is two words, but one phrase, so you need only one symbol for it. "Latest model? How about the outline of a female model? You know, lots of curves." So "Latest model" translates into ⟨⟩

"In perfect condition" . . . What are you going to do about that phrase? "How about a blue ribbon, like they award to first-prize winners at fairs and such?" Okay, so "in perfect condition" becomes ✿

124

"Delivered to my home" is also one phrase. It needs just one symbol. "How about a hand, showing that I'm getting something?" Well, a hand is a rather well-known symbol, but in this case we can accept it. Thus, "delivered to my home" becomes

"The ownership papers in my name," even though it talks about papers and your name, is also one phrase, one complete thought. Give me a symbol for it. "Well, the thing means a legal paper, so how about a symbol of the scales of justice?" Why not, providing we make it rather stylized. So "the ownership papers in my name" will look like this:

The last phrase: "by the end of this year." "That's easy. To me, the end of the year is always a dramatic time of completing things. Like they do in books, I always see it as an exclamation point." Let's put it on a slant, though, so it doesn't quite look like the standard symbol. And so "by the end of this year" becomes

Now, on a sheet of *scrap paper* draw the pentagram symbol shown in Figure 7:

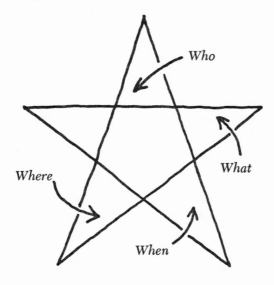

*Figure 7.*

Insert the words *Who, What, When,* and *Where* as above. Make your drawing large enough so that you can easily fit all the symbols of your sentence into the correct points.

At the top point, where it says "Who," draw in the symbol you used for "I." *Who* is you, right? So in that point goes "I."

The next symbol is "Blue." As it is part of *what* you want, you put that symbol into the point marked "What."

Now comes "Cadillac." It is also *what* you want, so it also goes into the "What" point along with "blue."

"Latest model" also belongs in the "What" point.

"In perfect condition" is still referring to the car itself, so it, too, goes into the "What" point.

"Delivered to my home" is *where* you want this to take place, so you should draw that symbol in the point marked "Where."

"The ownership papers in my name" is also *what* you want, so it gets drawn into the "What" point.

"By the end of this year" is *when* you want this carried out. Thus, the last symbol is drawn into the "When" point.

This done, you will notice that there is still one point of the pentagram that has not been filled in. It is that point to the left, between "Who" and "Where." This is a very important point because a great deal depends on *why* you want this new blue Cadillac latest model in perfect . . . etc. *Why* should "they" grant this wish to you? *Why* do you deserve it?

"Well," you reason, "if I have this new Cadillac I can take my children to school, I can get to work faster and feeling a lot better, and it will impress my neighbors that I must be doing something right."

So you want it only for show? "Oh no, but it would give me a new sense of importance in myself, that I was capable of doing bigger and better things with my life."

Okay, good answer. So now you need a symbol meaning "A new sense of importance in my life."

"How about three circles linked together, showing that I understand I am flesh, intellect, and spirit?"

Beautiful! So in the point marked "Why" you draw: ⟨OOO⟩

Now get yourself a large sheet of white paper. I prefer the shiny poster board that they sell in art supply houses. It can be any size, but two feet by three feet is about right.

Get some black ink—no colored inks, please. You don't want

to make one symbol more important than any other, and black on white is the strongest combination you can have. Now draw your pentagram so that it fills the paper. Draw *only* the outlines of it; do not put in the words "Who," "What," "When," "Where," and "Why."

Now draw in your symbols, as you have them on the scratch paper, and put them in the appropriate points of the pentagram. Based on the original sentence about the blue Cadillac, your pentagram should look like Figure 8.

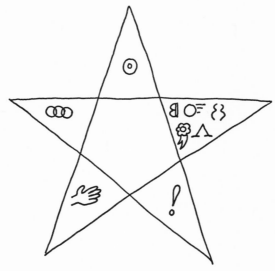

*Figure 8.*

Hang this *on a wall* in your home or office, in a room that you frequent a lot, or else in a hallway where you will pass by it several times a day.

Each time you go by this pentagram, or look up at it from your desk or the kitchen sink, look at it and *mentally understand* what each of those symbols means.

If you speak a foreign language, you will know what I mean. People who speak another language do not stop and translate each word into English. They hear a word and *know* what it means. There is no time lost in converting it back into their own native English. For instance, the Spanish word *casa*. Most of us know that *casa* means house, but those who speak Spanish as a second language understand—on a gut level—that *casa* is house. They hear *casa* and they immediately know what those four letters represent.

That's what you must do with your pentagram. You must be so used to seeing those symbols that you look at them and understand—without translating—that 🔲 means "blue," that ➰ means "delivered to my home," and 🌼 is "in perfect condition."

And—very important—while this is on your wall you will undoubtedly have many people asking you what it means. *Don't tell them.* Don't tell anyone! Not even your wife/ husband/children/mother/father. *Do not tell anyone what you are doing* and *never* translate any of the symbols of your pentagram for someone else! Not even *one* little symbol! To do so will take much-needed energy from your project, and this project needs energy, as you will see in a minute. To do so will also bring down derision and negativity. "You really think you're going to get a new Cadillac with that dumb thing?" or "Come on, don't be silly! That stuff doesn't work!" Don't let others into your projects, and they won't be able to explode them with their negativity. Believe me, I know of what I speak. Now go back and reread this entire paragraph to make sure that you understand what I'm saying!

When the day comes that you feel you have complete mastery of the symbols on the chart, and you are in complete command of your own emotions, and you are in a 100 percent positive frame of mind, then stand in front of the pentagram.

Do the Cosmic Forces three times. *Bring in all the energy you can handle. Really fill yourself with the force. Make sure your entire body is vibrating with the force and with the desire to have that blue Cadillac.*

Then, placing *your finger* on each symbol in turn, read each one *in a loud voice:*

*"I want a blue Cadillac, latest model and in perfect condition, delivered to my home, the ownership papers in my name, by the end of this year because I need a new sense of importance in my life!"*

Say it *once,* say it aloud. Say it with all the energy and emotion you can put behind it!

Now take the diagram off the wall, tear it up, and throw it

away. Throw the scraps in somebody else's garbage pail or in the river or in an abandoned lot. Forget about it. Forget that you want that Cadillac. Forget that you don't have the money to buy it. Forget that you ever asked for it in the first place! Go on about your normal daily business, but all the time your Sub-Conscious and your Super-Conscious will be working to give you that blue Cadillac in just the terms you set down and by the end of the year. Don't doubt it. Don't even think about it. If you have done it correctly, you'll get your car.

Now what have you done? You have taken energy and you have *created*—you have *forced*—a situation into being. What you have done has been done since time immemorial. If you'll dig back into any of the ancient books on spells, hexes, and charms, you'll see that all of them were based on *energy*. The amount of energy that was expended on them was in direct proportion to how well they worked. Read them and you'll see that they demanded the eye of a frog, the wing of a dried bat, a hair from the head of a virgin, a nail from a suicide's coffin or whatever.

It took a great deal of energy to locate all these things. It took *concentrated effort* to find these objects, and it took time. All the while the spell maker was thinking of the final result, the end product of his desire. All the time he was gathering virgin's toenails and prostitute's rosaries, he was thinking only of his desired object.

Then he would take these things to a witch, or a voodoo priestess, or a sorcerer, and that person would toss them into a pot, usually at midnight on a Friday the 13th (the waiting for the time and the exact date only increased the desire—that is, *the energy*). Finally, with much chanting (energy), much dancing (energy), much candle burning and incense smoking (energy again), the final moment came and with a gigantic burst of emotion (still more energy) the spell was cast.

You are doing the same thing with the pentagram. First you decide on what you really want—your decision takes energy. Then you write it out in such a way that there are no loose ends—that reflecting and examining time takes energy. Then you have to translate the words into symbols (more energy). Then you have to go out (energy) and get a new sheet of white paper, come back home (energy) and draw (energy) the pentagram. You pin it on the wall, pass it several times a week (energy), and finally call upon the Cosmic Forces, fill yourself with the energy, and—out loud (more energy)—you zap the words and the desire. When it has been done, you are exhausted; the message has been sent. The paper on which it was printed means nothing any more. It is destroyed. You do not think any more about it because to do so would only add static to the energy you have already sent. Let it go, pure and strong. Don't tamper with it any longer. Don't dilute the *energy.*

# LESSON 14
# Automatic Writing

When it comes to automatic writing, I am rather ambivalent —because while I have personally experienced the phenomenon, and have had excellent firsthand reports on messages obtained by others through this technique, I have also seen and read a lot of utter nonsense.

The messages that some have purported to receive from "spirits" have been so full of common platitudes that you wonder why the spirits bother wasting ink and paper. Some have been full of names, dates, and facts that when checked out proved completely worthless and invented. Why *spirits* would invent something is beyond me, especially if they know that the inventions will be investigated afterward. A message will come from your Aunt Maude, for instance, telling you things you already know and that you really weren't concerned about in the first place. Onto the paper will come the words, "Remember the nice day we had that lovely lunch?" What day? What lunch? Since you and Aunt Maude lived together for thirty-five years and had lunch together every day, you would think she could be a little more specific. Even if she adds, "and I spilled mustard on my new dress," it doesn't mean much. You were there, you witnessed the mustard hitting Maude's dress, and you filed it away in your Sub-Conscious. The fact that it has been jarred loose again does not necessarily mean that Maude is back and controlling your hand, but that you have "asked" the Little Man for contact with Aunt Maude and he is digging up all the trivia he has filed away on the old gal.

But suppose you get the message "Remember the nice day we had that lovely lunch and I spilled mustard on my dress? Well, that was the night I slipped out of the house and had an affair with Mr. Brown." Now, if you knew about the lunch and the mustard but not about Mr. Brown (after all, Aunt Maude was quite a swinger), you would not have had that information stored in your Sub-Conscious. And if you went to Mr. Brown with this bit of information, and he said, "Yes. Maude came over here that night still wearing the dress with the mustard stain on it, but we never told anyone," *then* you can consider that you have had direct communication with something outside your own mind level.

I say "something" because I don't know what it really is that gives us this type of information. The Spiritualists call it "evidence of survival," but I often wonder about that. I have a nagging theory in the back of my mind that maybe—just maybe—the spirit of Aunt Maude *cannot* contact the living again, ever, but that in order to contact us, and *make us pay attention,* the energies, the universal intelligence, and the Cosmic Forces *pretend* they are Aunt Maude. Therefore, we listen. I have discussed this with some of the most respected mediums and Spiritualist leaders in the world and none of them really knows if it is Aunt Maude or not. They find my theory interesting, but unsettling—as do I.

My own experiences with automatic writing haven't helped me clarify the issue. The first time I ever tried automatic writing was in Brazil. I had been reading about it in a local magazine and decided to make an experiment. I took a large pad of paper and a ball-point pen and, after placing the point of the pen on the paper, I covered my eyes with my left hand and let the right hand do its own thing. In a few minutes I had progressed past the squiggle-and-circle stage and started to get a message. It was in English, and it was full of platitudes like "There is no death" and "We are watching over you," etc.

After about three pages of this basic philosophy, I began to have my doubts about it all. Was it *me* or was it an outside force? Was this introductory lesson in Spiritualism coming from my own mind or from "spirit"? As those thoughts went through my mind, the pen, which had been racing across the paper, suddenly flew from my hand with such force that it broke into pieces when it hit the wall. I was so stunned, and my wrist ached so from this unexpected and brutal gesture, that I didn't try automatic writing again for months.

The next time I did so, it was against my will. I was in Los Angeles researching my book *The Psychic World of California* and one night, for lack of anything else to read before going to bed, I began the paperback edition of Diane Kennedy Pike's *Search,* the story of how her husband had perished in the desert of Israel as he searched for archeological clues to bolster his faltering belief in Christianity. I had already read a condensed version of the book in a magazine and wasn't impressed with it at all, but this time, as the hours went by, I found the book so fascinating and compelling that I was unable to put it down. The condensed version had taken all the personality from the book and I was delighted that I had at last been able to get the full flavor of Mrs. Pike's story.

AUTOMATIC WRITING

When I finally turned off the light it was very late, I had an early morning appointment so I wanted to get right to sleep. I had just punched the pillow and pulled up the covers when I heard a voice inside me say, "Get up and get a paper and pen."

I'm afraid that even after all the years I've been in this field, I don't always snap to it whenever I get instructions. Instead of jumping out of bed, I said, "Oh, no. I'm tired and I'm going to go to sleep!"

"Get out of bed and get some paper and a pen!" This time the order was louder and much firmer.

"Okay," I muttered, and turned on the light, sleepily found several sheets of typing paper and a ball-point pen. I sat on the edge of the bed, with the paper beside me, and put the pen in my right hand. Then I put the pen to the paper, turned my face away with a yawn, and hoped that whatever it was would be quick.

It was. The pen raced across the paper. There was some underlining and in the very end several exclamation points. Then, after many pages had been filled, the pen stopped.

I looked at the pages and couldn't believe it. It was a message to Mrs. Pike from her late husband. He wanted her to know several things and to consider several other points. The letter was very personal, almost a love letter. The exclamation points at the end were instructions to me: "Send this message to her!! Tell her I love her!! TELL HER!!!!"

I didn't tell her—not right away. For several days I debated whether or not to send the letter. First of all, I didn't know if the message was really from her late husband or was a super-figment of my imagination after having just finished her excellent book. Second, the lady had suffered greatly with the death of her husband and I didn't want to add more salt to her wounds. Third, we were both writers for Doubleday, and I didn't want her to comment to my editors that I was a complete kook. But I showed the letter to a few highly trusted friends in Los Angeles, professional mediums and psychics, and they all advised me to send it to Mrs. Pike. Finally I did, but with an even longer letter of my own explaining how I had gotten the message and under what circumstances—in other words, trying to leave as many exits open as possible.

In a few days I received a lovely letter from Mrs. Pike, thanking me very much for the message. While there were two points in it she didn't understand, she said, it was definitely in the style of her late husband and concerned certain things that only he would have known. I breathed a sigh of relief. I will always cherish her reply.

Now let's try it.

First get a small stack of white paper or a spiral notebook. You may have to experiment to see which you eventually prefer. You'll find that the stack of paper tends to slip off the desk after a while, but with the notebook you may be annoyed by having to turn each page flat before going on to the next one.

Get a pen that feels comfortable when you hold it. I prefer the ball-point to the new "felt tip" style because the ball rolls easier across the paper. Don't use a pencil—lead breaks under pressure.

Get *comfortably* seated at a desk or table. Make sure you've cleared the surface of any objects, like salt and pepper shakers, that your hand would be liable to bump into.

Arrange the papers in a neat pile (or place your notebook) at a comfortable distance from the edge of the table and a comfortable distance from your arm. In other words, don't place the paper so close to your body that you have to bend over to write on it, or so far away that you have to stretch your arm to reach it.

Pick up the pen in the hand that you normally use to write with. *Hold it easily:* not too tightly and not too loosely. You should hold it with just enough grip to know it's there, but firmly enough so that it doesn't wobble between your fingers.

Put the tip of the pen at the top of the first page. Turn your face away (or put your other hand over your eyes) and wait. Yes, wait.

Wait for a movement from the pen. *Do not force a movement.* Wait for the pen to move by itself. Your hand will be around it, your hand will be holding it; but your hand is there only to support the pen, *not* to force it to form letters and words. It's almost like ballroom dancing: The pen leads, you follow.

The first time you try this, you may not get anything at all. I'm not saying that to discourage you—I'm just telling you what to expect.

You need patience. You need to believe. You need to block all thoughts from your Conscious Mind that you want words to come from that lifeless pen over there. Think of buying a new suit, think of the movie you saw last week, of the steak you ate the other day, of the argument you had with your boyfriend—think of anything, anything but that pen waiting on the clean white paper. Even when your hand starts to move, *do not consciously think about what is being written.* It's difficult, I'll admit, but let your hand do it all by itself!

The first time you will probably get something that looks like this:

After a while it will look like this:

Then, if you are doing it correctly, it should begin to look like this:

Finally, when the channel is open and the message is coming through, it will look like ordinary handwriting. Do not be too surprised if it doesn't look like *your* handwriting!

Once you have done this several times, you'll be able to slip directly into the handwriting, without getting all the scribbles and circles first. You may want to set up a certain time each day for this and begin to fill a notebook with the information that is "coming through." For some reason, once the channel has been opened, "the other side" likes some orderliness and seems to work better if you can be contacted at the same time each day. Don't ask me why; I don't know. Ask the spirits!

If you get nonsense, stop writing. Put down the pen and *tell* them you think it's nonsense. That might end the session for the day, but it might also give them time to come in with another intelligence who knows what he's doing. I won't try to explain the spirit world—this isn't the place. But, it is the place to *know* that there is a force out there (whether it's Aunt Maude is something else again), and that you can contact this force through automatic writing. *It is one more form of mediumship.*

Don't get yourself all worked up about the information that's being given. I knew a woman who sold her home and moved into a hotel because the messages told her she was in the path of a tornado and the house would be destroyed. There was no tornado. She has no home.

Another lady, in Oregon, kept getting the message that her husband was going to die. It so upset her that she herself became ill and almost died. Her husband now forbids her to practice automatic writing, and rightly so, I think.

Entire books have been written about the messages from the "spirit" world that come via automatic writing: how some of the spirits are good and intelligent while others are evil and mischievous. If you feel that you need to be "protected" before you try this, then bring in the Cosmic Forces and surround yourself with the White Light. If what you get frightens you, stop immediately. But do this correctly and you will be open for all the other mediumistic experiences. Remember: *Listen.*

# LESSON 15

# Seeing Others' Past Lives

I'm always asked if I believe in reincarnation. I never hesitate in my answer: Yes.

If you have a chance, pick up some of the case histories in reincarnation done by Dr. Ian Stevenson and published by the American Society for Psychical Research in New York City. Dr. Stevenson, a sharp man not easily fooled, has spent the best part of his life tracking down children who claim to have lived before. He doesn't just write a few letters but actually gets on a plane and flies to India and Brazil and Australia to interview the children and their parents. Then he digs into the life the child claims to have led. His research would be fascinating reading for all of you.

I also suggest that you buy *The Infinite Boundary* by Guy L. Playfair and read about the woman in Brazil who recalled a life she had led as a prostitute in a brothel in Pompeii. Incredible stuff, and Playfair has done his homework well.

I have personal knowledge of two cases of reincarnation. The first was that of a woman (an astrologer!) who lived in San Francisco. She liked children but didn't care too much for men, so she figured out a way to get a baby without all the other stuff that had to go before it. Going into the red-light district, she found a pregnant prostitute. The girl had had three abortions and had been told by her doctor that if she had another one it would probably kill her. The astrologer said that she would be willing to pay all the girl's medical bills and hospital costs if she would turn the infant over to her when it was born. The prostitute agreed. A healthy baby boy was delivered and given to the astrologer.

The child had a normal first year and a pretty normal second year until he started to talk. He did the goo-goo and the ma-ma bit (after all, there was no da-da around), making sounds and fooling with single words like milk and cookie and all that kid stuff. Then one day, while his astrologer mother was with several friends in the living room, he marched in and stood before her. Then he uttered his first full sentence—a mind-blower. "I'm glad you're my mother in this lifetime," he said, "because you've been my mother in so many lifetimes before." Then he went back to his toys, leaving a shaken group in the living room.

The other story I know from personal investigation took place in a small Ohio town. A young mother had a five-year-old child named Richey. Ever since Richey's birth she had wanted another child, but each time she became pregnant she would lose the baby in a matter of weeks. This time, however, the baby inside her had been growing normally. Then one awful day she realized that it was no longer alive. She went to her doctor, who agreed with her that the fetus, about four months old, showed no signs of life. Naturally upset, the woman suggested that they give it a little more time: Maybe it would start to live again, maybe the tiny heart would resume beating. The doctor agreed to let her keep it for a few more days, but if there was no sign of life, she would have to have an operation that quite possibly would forever end her chances of bearing any other children.

A few days later, Richey was at his grandparents' farm. He had climbed up on the stone wall of a deep well and was doing a balancing act near the edge. His grandmother looked out the kitchen window and started for the door to tell him to get down from the wall, when he lost his footing and plunged to the bottom of the well. The grandmother looked at the clock on the wall (to this day she doesn't know why) and saw that it was 2:20 in the afternoon.

In her own home, about thirty miles away, Richey's mother felt the fetus inside her move! There was a thump and a stirring. Delighted, she glanced at the clock so that she could tell her doctor exactly when the child had begun to show signs of life. The time: 2:24 in the afternoon.

Shortly after that, her mother called and told her of Richey's accident. The child was dead; there had been no way to save him. The young mother collapsed and was rushed, in shock, to the hospital. Doctors were afraid that she would lose the baby she was carrying, but the unborn child continued to grow. Richey's grandfather, terribly upset and blaming himself for the boy's death, destroyed the walls of the well and filled in the hole. He wanted nothing standing that would remind him of the accident.

The woman had her baby, a healthy boy whom she named Charles. She gave him a great deal of love and affection, yet deliberately never told him that he had had an older brother. She thought she would wait until he was old enough to understand about death; and she herself didn't want to be reminded of the death of her firstborn.

One afternoon when Chuckie was almost three, his mother called him in for dinner. When he came into the house, he was looking at her in a quizzical way. "Why do you call me Chuckie?" he asked her. "My name is Richey."

Stunned, she asked him what he was talking about.

"Don't you remember?" he said. "I was at Grandpa's and was walking on that stone wall and I fell in."

She questioned Chuckie, but he swore that no one had told him anything. He *remembered* it, he insisted. She took him to the farm and he walked right to the spot where the well had been. "Here is where I fell," he said. "I died down there. In the water. I was wearing a red and white checked shirt and brown corduroy pants. Don't you remember, Mama?"

She remembered only too well, and she is positive that the two children are, in reality, one individual. After three or four years, Chuckie forgot about being Richey and has never mentioned it again.

If this story can be believed, it means that Richey's soul took exactly *four minutes* to reincarnate!

It seems to me the only fair way God could have handled things. We come into the world and we go through various learning processes in childhood, in formal schooling, in the business world, in the married world. And then, when we finally have a little bit of common sense, we are picked off in old age and lowered into the ground. It doesn't make sense that *that* is the end of it all. It seems an awful waste of time and energy and, especially, knowledge. It's like writing a book, getting it printed, and then destroying all the copies before the knowledge inside can be of any use; or like learning how to bake a delicious apple pie but never getting the chance to taste it.

That's why I believe in reincarnation. I don't believe that God is so wasteful that he would snuff out all the knowledge that each human has amassed over a lifetime. I believe that we come back—and come back again and again—with most of our experiences in past lives on call when we need them in *this* life. I like to point to child prodigies who play the violin at five, play chess at six, write novels at ten. If we know only what we have picked up in this lifetime, then from *where* has the prodigy received his knowledge? If the Creator in His infinite wisdom (as the Bible terms it) is really on the ball, He surely makes use of the learnings from one life to enrich the next.

Now let's get to *work*.

In order to see someone else's past life you have to have someone else to look at, right? So this is another exercise in which you should have a partner. People always seem more interested in what they have been than in what they are going to be. They know the present, are making plans for the future, but past lives remain much more exciting and mysterious.

Again, the less well you know your partner, the better. If you know him too well you may have heard him express ideas such as: "I've always liked Chinese food. I must have been in China in a past life," or "English history fascinates me. I must have lived over there at one time." This type of preconditioning can put you off. So choose someone you don't really know that well.

Remember how you built up the communications link before by sitting face to face and holding hands? Okay, I want you to do the same thing this time, except that I don't want you to hold hands. Turn the lights way down low, or turn them off. Light a candle and place it on the floor, or on a side chair, so that the light throws illumination on the face of your partner.

The one who is being read (that is, whose lives will be seen) should close his eyes and start down the color rainbow.

See *Red* . . .

*Orange* . . .

*Yellow* . . .

*Green* . . .

*Blue* . . .

*Lilac* or *Violet.*

When he has reached *Violet* or *Lilac* he should surround himself in that color, see his entire body enveloped in that color, and *know* he is in his Alpha Level.

Then he is to walk down that marble corridor until he comes to the staircase. Next he is to go down the stairs—remember there are twenty-one in all—until he comes to the bottom landing.

Now he is to go to the door of his Secret Place, open that door, and enter. He is to find himself a comfortable position in his Secret Place, relaxing and breathing easily.

Once he is relaxed in his Secret Place, he is mentally to ask that his past lives *appear on his physical face*. He is to tell his Little Man to parade the various lives he has lived across his features. His past faces are to be superimposed upon his present-life face.

*All of this is to be done in complete silence,* with you sitting across from him, waiting.

When he has reached the Secret Place and has asked for his past faces to be shown he will tell you: "Okay."

That's all the speaking he is to do.

Now close your eyes, almost to a squint. Close your eyes so that you will have to lift your head to see your partner's face through your eyelids. Silently stare at his face.

What do you see? There will be shadows, of course, from the candle, and visibility will be difficult, but concentrate on his face.

See his features change.

See the eyes get larger or smaller.

See a beard where there was none before.

See the skin get darker or lighter.

See the face go from youth to old age.

See the transformation that is coming over your partner's face.

Don't speak. Don't tell him anything that you see. Keep the silence.

After several minutes of this you can tell your partner, "Okay," and he will mentally leave his Secret Place, close the door, come back up the stairs, walk down the corridor, and go from *Lilac* up into *Blue*.

Up into *Green* . . .

Up into *Orange* . . .

Up into *Red* . . .

He opens his eyes. He is back.

Now you can tell him what you saw. Don't be embarrassed or inhibited. Describe everything fully: the color of his hair, a scar, gold earrings, or a pirate's kerchief. Whatever you saw, describe it fully. As you do this, he will tell you if he can relate to anything you've seen:

"Wow! In a nun's habit! I always wanted to be in the Church!"

"Large blue eyes and yellow hair! I've always dreamed of

having those things instead of the brown eyes and black hair I have!" And so on.

In Mexico City, one male student disappeared before the eyes of his partner! I was hastily summoned and the partner whispered: "Look at him, tell me what you see."

I looked, but I didn't see a head. All I could see was his shoulders and shirt collar.

"Exactly," said the partner. "That's all I can see too!"

When the student came back up through the colors, we told him what we both had seen. He was amazed. "I've always had this thing for France," he said, "and I just *know* that I was there during the Revolution. And I always suspected that I had been decapitated in the guillotine. Look at this birthmark." He turned around and pulled down the back of his shirt collar. There was a thin red line running straight across the back of his neck!

# LESSON 16

# Astral Travel

Astral travel, or an out-of-body experience, can be a real trip! With very little practice, once you have the right techniques you can go anywhere you choose and report on anything or anyone firsthand. It's not scary either—not the way I do it and not the way you will do it.

A businessman in Virginia named Robert Monroe wrote a great book on his astral trips called *Journeys Out of the Body*. He found his trips frightening because he didn't know what was happening and because his adventures always took place when he was asleep—in other words, when his Conscious Mind was not in control . . . at least not in the beginning. I'll show you a way to take the same kind of trips and yet be wide-awake and in complete control at all times.

As I've said repeatedly, no matter what the exercise, you must be in control of your Conscious Mind at all times. Just because you've set it aside doesn't mean you aren't in control of it. The fact that you have pushed it away to listen to your Sub-Conscious or Super-Conscious Mind proves that you have it where you want it. It's over there in a corner, but *you've* put it there.

This is as good a time as any to talk about drugs and other mind-boggling outsiders like pot, alcohol, tobacco, and pills. You cannot control any of the three levels of your mind if you are "high" on outside stimulants. The reason that so many people freak out on LSD is that the drug grabs their Conscious and Sub-Conscious mind levels and races off with them. It takes them for a "trip" that's like being tied up with ropes in the back seat of your own car with some maniac in the driver's seat. It's still your car, and you're still inside it, but you've no control over the wheel.

In order to do anything with your mind levels, you have got to be in control.

So before you start on any type of astral projection, I don't want you to have smoked a cigarette (regular, filtered, or potted). I don't want you to have taken a drink of booze or even a cup of coffee—Sanka is okay, but regular coffee is a no-no, since the caffeine in it takes away some of your control. Abstain from any of the above for at least *three* hours. Give the stimulants in any tobacco, alcohol, or coffee you may have had before then time to work themselves out of your nervous system.

If you think that you *must* have a cigarette, or that you can't last three hours without a cup of coffee, then why bother with anything in this course at all? Obviously you are not in command of your own mind, the nicotine or caffeine is. Be a slave to the tobacco and coffee industry if you must, but don't tell me or anyone else that you've got yourself together—because you haven't.

I knew a woman in Brazil who walked out on her husband because he wanted to play the macho role all the time and insisted that she follow his orders. She told him that she was her own boss and didn't have to take orders from anyone or anything. She related the entire domestic epic to me between cups of black coffee and half a pack of cigarettes. No sir, she was in complete command of herself and don't let anyone think differently!

Okay, assuming that you've abstained for three hours from all stimulants, let's get ready to take a trip.

First, look at a clock and make a mental note, or write it down if you will, as to when you started your trip. This is so you can check later on all details involving time.

Take off your shoes and loosen your belt. I don't want anything tight or restricting on your body. That means wristwatches and any costume jewelry rings (wedding bands may have been there for so long that many of you no longer feel them—let alone recall their significance).

Also stifle any ticking alarm clocks and turn off all radios and hi-fi's. You should be in as close to absolute silence as possible. Granted, in this day and age it's difficult to get completely away from such noises as automobiles and voices of next-door neighbors, but *try* to pick a place that is as sound-proof as possible. If there is a telephone around, either turn it off or take the receiver out of the cradle and smother it with several pillows. And, for goodness sake, if there is anyone else in the house with you, tell them *not* to come into the room! This is most important! Just locking your door is not enough. Tell them that you do not want to be disturbed for *any* reason. Tell them so they won't come tapping at your closed door or jiggling the door knob. If you live with someone who thinks all this is batty to begin with, and they ask you what you're going to be doing, tell them you're going to paint your toenails—a job that requires meticulous attention—or that you're going to perform brain surgery on your grandmother. Tell them *anything* so long as you're not disturbed.

Now dim the lights in the room, but leave *some* light on—I don't want you returning to your body in the dark. Lie down on the floor. Lie down in an open area where you will not be touching any piece of furniture or any other person. (Don't lie down on a bed. The odds are five to one that you'll fall asleep rather than take a trip.) If more than one person is doing this with you, make sure you don't touch his or her physical body in any way. The slightest jolt or physical sensation could cause you to come careening hastily back into your body and could— just *could*—cause a minor physical or emotional upset.

Now count down through the rainbow of colors. Begin with the color red and go all the way down and into violet or lilac. *See* these colors and go down and into each one of them as you have previously been doing.

When you have reached the color violet think about the place you wish to visit. Maybe you want to go to a friend's house on the other side of town. Maybe you want to travel to see a relative who is living thousands of miles away. Maybe you want to check on what your ex-husband is doing. No matter where you choose to go—at least for the first few times you take these trips—*choose a place where you have already been physically.* Choose a place that you *know*. Don't try to get into Raquel Welch's bedroom on your first flight.

Now that you have chosen one place to visit and your mental body has reached the violet Alpha Level, ready your physical body for the trip.

In this state of complete mental relaxation, picture the big toe on your *left* foot and concentrate on it. That's right, the big toe on your left foot. *See* it in your mind's eye. See it down there under your sock. If you must, wiggle it to get a more physical image of it. Now, once you have it firmly pictured in your mind, *make it tingle.*

That's right, send all your thought energy down to it and make it tingle. Make it feel as if it's being attacked by a thousand tiny needles. *Feel* it. Become aware of it. Your entire mental effort is being directed toward this big toe. Don't be discouraged if the tingling doesn't come right away. Keep your thoughts and mental energies on that toe and it will start to tingle, I promise you.

Now, once it is tingling, keep it tingling while you concentrate upon the big toe of your *right* foot. Do the same thing with this big toe that you did with the other toe. Picture it. Wiggle it if you must in order to locate it, but send all your mental effort to that big toe. *Make this toe tingle.* Keep at it until it does.

You should now have both big toes tingling.

Go back to your *left* foot. Concentrate upon the *toes* of your *left* foot. That big toe is already tingling, so make all the toes on that foot tingle in the same way. See them. *Know* they are there. *Make them tingle.* You'll be surprised how quickly they fall into line with the tingling big toe.

Okay, once those toes are tingling, direct your attention to the toes of your *right* foot. Do the same with them as you did with your left ones. *Make them tingle,* really tingle! Now feel this sensation running across the toes of *both* feet. The toes of both feet are *united* by the same tingling energy sensation.

With your toes all aglow, go back and concentrate upon the *sole* of your *left foot. Make it tingle.* When you feel it tingling, concentrate upon the *sole* of your *right foot. Make it tingle.* Now the *top* of your *left foot.* Now the *top* of your *right foot.* Now your *left ankle.* Now your *right ankle.*

Both your feet are now tingling, from the toes up to the ankles. *Now bring this sensation up the calves of both legs.* Bring the tingling *up both legs* at the *same time. See* your calves in your mind's eye. *Feel* your calves receiving the tingling sensation from your feet.

Your feet are still tingling. Moving the energies upward has not diminished the tingling sensation of your feet. All it has done is spread the energies higher. And now your feet and calves are tingling together.

Now up to your *kneecaps. Feel* them tingle.

Now up through your *thighs.* Up both thighs to your hips. *Feel* your thighs tingle.

Now the tingling sensation comes up into your *abdomen.*

Now up into your *stomach.*

Now up into your *chest.*

Now up into and across your *shoulders.*

Now feel the fingers of your *left hand* begin to tingle.

Now feel the *fingers* of your *right hand* begin to tingle.

The tingling sensation rushes up your *left arm* into your left shoulder.

The tingling sensation rushes up your *right arm* into your right shoulder.

Your entire body from the soles of your feet to your shoulders is now tingling. You can feel the energy. It is there. *It is real.*

Bring the energy upward now, into your *throat*. Make your throat tingle with this upward surge of energy.

*Now up into your face.* Feel your *chin*, your *lips*, your *nose*, your *eyes*, and your *forehead* tingling.

You've now reached the point of departure. Pay attention to the sensations from now on.

Bring the tingling sensation up to your *scalp*. Feel your *scalp* tingling.

Your entire body is now tingling from the soles of your feet to the scalp of your head.

THINK OF THE PLACE YOU WISH TO VISIT.

GO THERE!

JUST LEAVE!

BON VOYAGE!


Shhhhh.

It is at this point that I, the instructor, must stand aside. In no way will I speak to you or give you guidance or instruction. I'll make no noises, I'll offer no advice. You are on your own now and must not be disturbed.

You will find that you have entered the place where your friend is. Maybe you came in through the door, but more likely you passed in through the walls. Possibly there was a rushing sensation in your ears as you left your body and overcame time and space. For that's what you have done, you know. You have transported yourself in an instant from the floor of your room into your friend's surroundings.

This should be one more proof of what I've been telling you all along: Time and space are man-made measurements. The Super-Conscious doesn't need them to function. The Super-Conscious refuses to be hemmed in by them.

Once you have arrived at your destination, look around and

see what's going on. Notice if anything is out of place or awry, such as the refrigerator door being open, the beds unmade, or the cat climbing the curtains. Look around this place and see it. You *will see it! Remember* what you see. That is important.

Also *see* what your friend is doing. Is he eating? Reading the newspaper? Watching television? Chatting on the phone? Remember what he is doing.

Is he alone or with someone? How are they sitting? Listen to see if you can pick up any of their conversation.

See if you can make your presence felt. Touch your friend on the arm or the forehead. Just reach out and touch him. Call his name. Call your own name several times. By that I mean *mentally* call, of course. Don't use your physical voice or make any physical movements whatsoever. Remember, you will not be inside your body. Your *physical self* will *not* be in that room across town. Your *astral* self will be there, and it communicates silently and effortlessly.

Take your time. There is no time. Make a mental note of how your friend is dressed, what he is doing, what the place looks like.

Then when you are ready—BUT ONLY WHEN YOU ARE READY—think of your body lying on the floor and think of returning to it.

*All you have to do is think of returning to your body and you will return.*

You will return quickly, effortlessly, immediately.

Remain on the floor for a few minutes with your eyes closed. Don't try to move around just yet. Lie there and feel your back and your legs on the hard floor.

Open your eyes. Sit up slowly. The trip is over.

If you are doing this with others in the room who are also on trips, *don't make any noises when you return.* Do not do anything to disturb anyone else in the slightest way. Don't talk; don't turn on the lights; and *please* don't touch them. When all the others have opened their eyes and are sitting up, then and *only* then can you begin to move around and speak. Even if it means sitting there for another fifteen minutes until everyone has checked back into their bodies, do it.

This is the time to go to your phone and call the friend you just visited. Ask him what he has been doing for the past half hour. Ask him what kind of clothes he is wearing. Find out if he is alone or with someone. *How does all this stack up with what you have just seen?* How well did you travel? What percentage of your vision was correct?

Naturally, he will start asking you questions. "Why do you want to know these things?" will be first on his list.

Tell him that you had been thinking of him and decided to call. Play it cool here, and *more often than not* he will remark that he had just been thinking of *you*. Of course, if he is himself interested in this field and believes some of it, your chances of getting through to him on a mental level are better. But even scoffers will find it "odd" that you should call them just after they had been *thinking* of you.

Carole Hedin lives in Hollywood, California, but her mother lives on a small island in Ontario, Canada. The mother doesn't have a phone and must drive ten miles to the general store if she wants to use one. Carole has the darndest time communicating with her because of this.

At the time of the class, Carole was planning a trip to Canada. She had already notified her mother the day she would arrive, but then something happened and Carole was forced to delay her flight by one day. Knowing that she didn't have time to send a letter, Carole decided to visit her mother on her astral trip.

"Momma, the plane will be a day late. I'll be there on Saturday," she told her. "Please don't get upset when you drive to the airport on Friday and I'm not on the plane." Carole said she repeated this at least six times. Then she added, "Is it okay if I bring Rufus?" Rufus is Carole's pet hound dog.

That evening, just to be on the safe side, she phoned the general store and asked to have someone deliver a message to her mother. "Is it about your plane trip?" the shop owner asked.

"Yes," came her startled reply.

"Well," said the man, "your mother came by here about an hour ago to say that if you called I should say she'd be at the airport on Saturday instead of Friday. She also said something about 'Thanks for your visit.' What does that mean?"

"I'll tell you later," Carole said, trying to hold back a laugh.

"Your mother also asked me to tell you to please not wear that blouse when you come to visit her." (Carole had been wearing a T-shirt in class with some rather suggestive lettering across the front. Her mother had never seen her in it.) "Oh, yes. Something about a dog. Said she'd love to see him again."

In one of my Los Angeles classes, a businessman named Tom Mitchell decided to leave his body and travel to his home. He had asked his wife to get some contracts together and mail them out that morning, and he wanted to make sure that she'd done so. Once he had zoomed through the air and arrived in his living room, he saw his wife watching television. "I was so angry with her," he told the class when we had all returned from our trips, "that I tried to grab her by the shoulders and scream at her to get those things in an envelope and take them to the post office. I went to the desk drawer and tried to open it so I could throw the papers at her feet. Nothing makes me angrier than when she promises to do things and doesn't!"

A half hour later, on the lunch break, he called his house and asked to speak to his wife. His daughter said that her mother wasn't home. "Where is she?" Tom demanded.

"At the post office," came the reply. "You know, Dad, I think Mother's been working too hard. She was in the living room watching television when all of a sudden she screamed, jumped up, and began to stuff some papers into an envelope. As she dashed out the door she said she was going to the post office and you'd kill her when you got home."

"When did all this happen?" Tom asked, delighted with himself.

"About a half an hour ago."

As if those two successful trips in the same class weren't enough, Helen Seboia and Pat Champion *met each other* on their astral trip. Unknown to either of them, they had chosen to visit the same mutual friend.

"I was amazed," Helen reported, "that no sooner was I in that house when Pat came flying in through the walls. I told her to get out, that this was *my* project. She asked me what I was doing on *her* trip! Then I became so angry that I flew away and went to visit someone that Pat doesn't know."

Pat confirmed everything Helen had said. The interesting thing was that when they phoned their mutual friend, the lady admitted she had "felt their presences" that morning and asked, "Why had Helen been so upset?"

None of these people—in fact no one in that class—had ever tried astral travel before.

It worked for them and it can work for you.

I think the main reason some people fail when they attempt such astral flights is fear that they won't be able to come back to their bodies. I have heard of a few cases in which persons were unable to *find* their bodies for a few seconds—and panic set in—but I don't know of anyone who didn't finally make it back.

Another reason so many fail is that they don't know how to prepare themselves for the trip in the first place. Now *you* know.

If you learn the basics of astral travel and understand that there is no real danger if all precautions are taken, you can do it any time at all. The ancients knew this, and so have all the "secret" societies.

Happy flying!

# LESSON 17

# Table Tipping

This is always a lot of fun, especially in a large class. And to terminal skeptics and congenital scoffers there is nothing more convincing than to see a table suddenly lift itself up on two legs and scurry across the room.

In the mid-1700s in France, a popular theme of discussion was "animal magnetism." Scientists of the day were trying to uncover the force that radiated from all things, animate or inanimate, and how it interacted with other forces. They called this force a "magnetic fluid." Everyone could see that there was *something* there. How else could you account for the fact that one piece of metal could be attracted and attached to another piece without being bolted or melted to it? And if you had a certain kind of metal, it would make a lady's hairpin jump off the table and cling to it. Now explain that—or the fact that if you ran your comb through your hair, small bits of paper would jump onto the comb?

Turning to the attraction between people, could it be that "love at first sight" was no more than two compatible fluids joining? (Hardly a very romantic notion, especially for the French!) And maybe the reason people were enemies was because their fluids didn't interact well. A dog doesn't like a cat. Why? Opposite fluids. Sugar and vinegar? Opposite fluids. The priest and the sinner? Their fluids. People were doing "magnetic" healings in other parts of Europe, actually curing ailments by sending their magnetic fluids in to mingle with the fluids of the person who was ill! What did it all mean, and how could it all be used?

Table tipping came into vogue in the mid-1800s, when society ladies discovered that if they had a congenial group of people at a dinner party, afterward they could all make a table rise and tap out messages by placing their hands on it. It was a lot more fun than hiring strolling gypsies to entertain—and a lot cheaper, too. Soon all of France was tipping tables.

A code was worked out. One tap of the table leg meant Yes, two taps meant No, three meant Maybe. That way they were able to spell out complete words and then complete sentences. A message would slowly come through. "Is it a B?" Two taps. "Is it an R?" One tap, and so it would continue.

The "spirits" that came through were unpredictable, representing various grades of intelligence and various historical epochs. Naturally, if you had an elegant group to dine, you would have preferred Cleopatra to come through with a message rather than Schultz the butcher, but you had to accept whoever it was. Messages became more personal. Departed Aunt Louise would be talking about Cousin Frederick. "Poor Frederick . . . died when kicked by a horse, you know. His wife never quite consoled herself." But then Frederick would come through and tap out messages telling where the family treasure had been hidden from the always-invading Germans, or what he thought of his daughter's future husband, or what the price of gold would be in a month's time. Even the Emperor, Napoleon III, was holding these amusing table-rapping sessions.

There was one man who was not amused though: a medical doctor named Hippolyte Rivail. He had taken a long time to learn medicine and all its accompanying arts and was annoyed that these tables pretended to have more medical knowledge than the universities had. He decided to investigate these silly sessions and unmask them for what they really were.

As always happens in cases like this, the man became converted by the very thing he set out to destroy.

Rivail hired a group of assistants to go around the fashionable salons where the table tipping was done and present a specific list of questions to the supposed spirits. Then the assistants would meet and compare the answers from the different tables. Of course, Rivail was positive, the answers would vary wildly from table to table.

But they didn't. Though the replies had been given at different times and dates and in different homes, and though some of the replies were given in down-to-earth language while others were adorned with quotations from classical Greek or the Latin philosophers, all the answers were substantially the same. Some spirits spoke to Dr. Rivail personally, admonishing him for trying to debunk "the truth." They even gave him a new name, asking him to use "Allan Kardek" when he wrote his report. He did and the name became the symbol for a brand-new religion eventually called Spiritualism. (Why these things always have to be turned into a *religion*, I've never quite understood.)

At approximately the same time, the Fox sisters rose to

prominence in the United States because of their table tippings and spirit rappings. It is doubtful whether Kardek or the Fox sisters knew of one another at the time.

These three young girls were living with their parents in a small rented farmhouse near Rochester, New York. One night, strange tappings were heard in their bedroom. Once they got over their fright, they tried to communicate with the maker of the noises by working out a code very similar to the one the French society matrons were using—one rap for Yes, two for No, three for Maybe, and so on. After a few nights, the message came through. The rapper was a salesman who had visited that farmhouse several years before, when another family lived there. The farmer had robbed the salesman of the money he had in his pockets, then killed him and buried his body in the cellar. The spirit even told the girls the exact location where his bones could be found.

When the girls told their parents about this, there was much ridicule and punishment for lying; Mr. and Mrs. Fox were not the most intelligent or kindly parents in the world. But finally the girls prevailed. The spot in the cellar was unearthed and there they found the skeleton of a man, accompanied by a salesman's valise.

The news got out and the entire countryside wanted to hear about it. The girls later went on to become great celebrities and to endure much unjust criticism.

Spiritualism reached its heyday in the early 1900s and then declined with the coming of World War I, dying out almost entirely by the 1930s. If you are at all interested in history and how things psychic have been dealt with, I strongly suggest that you read about this period in such fascinating books as *The Occult* by Colin Wilson, *The Mediums' Book* by Allan Kardek, *Modern American Spiritualism* by Emma Hardinge, and my own *Drum & Candle*.

Ever since Kardek and the Foxes, naturally, there have been people out to disprove that anything "supernatural" can happen to a table. They have claimed that a table moves because of "involuntary muscle reaction"—meaning (I think) that people so want to have the table move that their muscles start moving their fingertips without them being aware of it. Others have said that the table doesn't really move, but that the phenomenon is really one of mass hypnosis. (Yet photographs exist showing tables with all four legs off the floor. It's rather difficult to hypnotize a camera!) Still others claim that since the table chosen for use is usually very lightweight it's easy to shove around by one person who makes all the others think "spirits" are doing it.

Once in New York City, several years before I had seriously gotten into this field, I was invited to a party. After dinner, the hostess wanted to see if we could make the table move. The one she chose was a heavy old Victorian monster that five men had barely been able to carry up the stairs to her apartment. It stood on a heavy round base—in other words, it had no legs and no feet. By the time we finished, that table had moved all over the room and left great gouges in the hostess' polished hardwood floor.

Shall we get started?

I assume that you have a group ready, ideally four or more persons who are interested in seeing what can be done. You don't have to have an odd or even number around the table. That seems to be irrelevant. It simply seems that *collective* energy is needed to make a table move. I say "it seems," because I've never seen one person alone make a table rise up. I've seen *three*, but never less than that. But it does seem that the more people you have around a table, the better movement you will get. It's as if human bodies are used as batteries to capture the outside energy and focus it onto the table.

I've discovered several other things too. One is that not everyone at the table has to believe in a spirit world or even that this table stuff really works. Only one or two persons sitting there have to believe. Strange, and I wish I had the answer.

Another of my findings is that certain combinations of people work better together than others. Maybe there *was* something to the old idea of "fluids" and "animal magnetism," something that we should study and use in this "advanced" intellectual age we live in.

Especially for the first few experiments, choose a table that is not too heavy; the best table, in the beginning, is a card table.

It is light and easy to carry from place to place if you decide to continue your experiments at different homes.

Next, clear away any rugs on the floor. It is *always* better to do this experiment on a smooth wood or linoleum floor. The legs will glide better and you won't have to stop and untangle them from nap and fringe.

Move all the furniture in the room as far away from the table as possible. If you can do this in a large room that's completely free of other furniture, even better. You'll find this warning a word to the wise, because once the table starts moving you won't be able to control it completely, and you don't want it battering into a lamp or television set.

Place the right number of chairs around the table; if four people, four chairs. Make sure they're lightweight chairs because when the table *really* moves, you'll have to jump up with it and follow it. Chairs will have to be quickly shoved out of the way. But don't try to do this experiment standing up to eliminate the need for chairs. It will only tire your back as you bend over waiting for the action to begin, and sometimes you'll wait as long as twenty minutes, depending on the energies that have to be created.

Now choose a leader, the person who will be doing all the talking. This person should ideally have had some experience in table tipping, or at least have a firm belief that it will work.

Everyone sits at the table and places his or her hands *palms down* on the surface of the table. Place them close to the edge, but so the complete hand is flat on the surface. *Don't use a lot of pressure.* Let your palms sit comfortably on the table top.

There is a theory that everyone should be touching hands at this time; that your little finger should be up against the little fingers of the person to your right and to your left, to form a chain of energy. I have done table tipping both ways and whether fingertips are touching or not seems to make little difference. When the table actually starts to move, it's quite difficult to keep those little pinkies together.

Once everyone is seated, with hands on the table, the leader of the group says a prayer. It can be of any length, but is directed usually to the spirit world asking for protection and guidance and that the session be successful.

Then the leader asks: "Is there a spirit here?" and keeps asking this every few minutes until the table begins to move slightly. The others at the table keep quiet. Only the leader is to make any comments, at least in the beginning.

Soon, if everything is going well, there will be a wobble from the table. The leader will ask if there is a spirit present and, if there is, will he please move the table once for Yes.

When that movement is made, the leader asks if it is a "good" spirit or a "bad" spirit. Good spirits get one wiggle and the bad ones two.

Then the leader asks the name of the spirit. By starting with A and going down the line, you'll get a name spelled out— again, one tap for Yes and two taps for No.

Once you have the name, then you can start asking questions. The usual next question is: "Do you have a message for us?"

"Yes."

"For whom?"

The name of a person at the table is spelled out, or you can make it simpler by asking: "For Mary?" No. "For Tom?" No. "For Judy?" Yes. "Okay, let's start with the message. Does the first word begin with A? B?" and so on.

Sometimes the table won't want to spell out anything at all, or else the energies will get bored with the game and will start acting up.

Once, when my Hollywood class did this, the message was broken off when I went over to the table and demanded that it hurry because it was getting late and we all wanted to go home. The table suddenly rose up on two legs and came at me. I laughed and walked away. The table followed me, and those sitting around it had to shove their chairs back and walk quickly to keep their hands on top. Each time it got near me it would tilt up on two legs as if the other two wanted to embrace me. I could feel something there, inside the upturned legs, a type of energy that I have felt when I've reached into the insides of a tilted pyramid structure. Then the legs lowered and the table was silent.

"There's nobody there," I said. "Let's fold it up and go home." Then up it rose again, and I walked away, and it followed me. This happened for at least fifteen minutes with everyone in the room laughing and teasing me and the table.

The funny part of it was when a waiter came into the hotel room where we were having the class and almost dropped his tray when he saw what was happening. He stood there dumbfounded by the sight of a card table seemingly running around the room with a life of its own.

"If I hadn't seen it with my own eyes, I wouldn't have believed it," he kept saying. "If I hadn't seen it myself!"

There is no "danger" to any of this that I can see. You are always in control of the situation, and in order to stop the table, all you have to do is remove your hands. But once in Phoenix, Arizona, the table was moving around the room so fast that the students were unable to keep their hands on it. It moved for about *another six feet* under its own power!

In the words of that Hollywood waiter: "If I hadn't seen it with my own eyes . . ."

# THE ADVANCED COURSE

Now that you have come this far—and *if* you have done every-thing correctly—you are no longer a novice. There is really nothing you can't do. You can heal, do ESP, take an astral trip, get what you want from the pentagram, write automatically, tip a table, and make an impression on anyone anywhere in the world. It should all be easy for you now. Be truthful . . . it wasn't very difficult, was it?

Now I'm going to give you two segments that I always reserve for my advanced class—for those who have gone through all the rest and who are willing to come back for more. I put these under an "advanced" heading because they should be done only when you have mastered the rest. It's not that they are more difficult; it's that they require more profes-sionalism, more understanding, and a greater comprehension of the powers the human mind has. They also require that the student be more aware of his surroundings and be absolutely aware of the character and personality of those around him. They require vigilance and integrity. They should not be at-tempted unless you *understand yourself*. Socrates said, "Know thyself." I couldn't agree with the old boy more!

# LESSON 18

# Helping Others Into Their Past Lives

The technique I'm going to teach you now seems very simple—and that's part of the problem. It's so simple *on the surface* that many feel they can do it at once. They therefore start practicing on their friends without taking into consideration the dangers and the pitfalls inherent in the experience.

The exercise in which you watched your partner's face for indications of what past lives he or she had led was just a warm-up for the one I'm going to give you now. Nothing was expected of you then except pure reporting. Your role is more vital now, and you must be constantly on the alert.

When you take someone back into a past life by this method, you must not let down your guard for one minute. You must stay with the person and lead him along. You will not *guide* him, or even point the way. You will simply *accompany him as he takes himself* into his past existences. At no time must you leave him alone. At no time must you insist. At no time must you impose your own personality. The traveler needs you on these trips, but only as a novice swimmer needs a life jacket. He must swim ahead on his own, but with the knowledge that if the water gets too deep and treacherous you are always there to rescue him.

If I've frightened you, I'm sorry. If I've made you cautious about trying this, I'm glad. As you do this, you'll understand what I mean.

Shall we begin?

A person comes to you wanting to know about his past lives. He knows that you can take him back, he trusts you to lead him, and he expects more from you than he will get. You'll see.

When this person starts to tell you why he wants to go into his past, he will *invariably* tell you which of his past lives he wants to revisit. "I want to go back to the one where I was a priest in Atlantis," he'll say, or "I want to see where I was a soldier in the Civil War." Just smile at him, because the chances of his going to either of those lives—*if* he ever did live them—are about a hundred to one. Of all the past-life regressions I've ever done, *nobody* has ever gone to a life he or she *consciously* expected to visit. They have always gone back to existences they had no idea they had lived, and the shock (and delight) is always enormous.

*Never* promise someone you will take him to a definite life. You only accompany. You do not guide.

It's also good to make clear to the person, right from the outset, that you will not hypnotize him. He will be in control of himself at all times. He will not be under your influence. He will be listening to you, but he will be obeying his own instincts. This is important, because many people feel that under hypnosis they will be subject to all kinds of indignities from robbery to rape. Assure the person with whom you're working that he is in control and can revert to himself, in his present life, simply by wanting to do so.

Here, again, as in psychometry, personal readings, and healing, the person must *want* to be regressed. Don't force yourself on someone who is in doubt or who is afraid. Don't waste your energies and your time. If a person thinks this is all foolishness, don't try to convert him. Let him go on his way and bless him.

Have your person sit in a comfortable chair, facing you. If he feels better with his shoes off, fine. Make sure he's got things like notebooks and such off his lap and on the floor. He may want to tape his session. Fine—that way he can analyze what was said after he gets home.

Tell him that you are not going to hypnotize him. Tell him that all he has to do is open his eyes and he will be back with you. Tell him to relax, tell him there is nothing to worry about, tell him he is going to go on a marvelous trip.

There is a formula you *must* follow here. If the person who is being regressed has been studying this course with you, then the first part will be old hat to him and he'll slip easily into it. If not, you must go step by step—and you must tread carefully. *Each* step must be taken in the proper sequence to gain the proper effect. This is one time when improvisation is not advised.

Turn down the lights in the room. Most people don't like being in the dark, so leave one dim light burning in a far corner, giving the person the assurance that there is light somewhere if he needs it.

*Important:* have a glass of water ready and waiting near him.

Begin by asking the person—and this is very important if he hasn't been studying the course with you—to close his eyes and to *imagine* the place where he lives. Tell him to *see* his home or the building he calls home. When he *sees* it with his eyes closed, he is to tell you, "Yes, I see my house."

Okay, you say. Now, do you drive a car? "Yes." All right, I want you to see that car. I want you to see yourself walking over to your car and getting into it. *See* the car, *see* its color. Do you *see* it? "Yes."

Okay. Now I want you to see a circle. *See* it form inside your head, in the center of your forehead. It can be a hollow circle or it can be solid. It can be any color you wish. Do you see it? "Yes."

Fine. Now I want you to erase the circle and in its place I want you to see a cross. *See* the form of a cross in your mind. *See* it there inside your forehead. *See* it in your mind's eye. Do you *see* it? "Yes."

Fine. Now I want you to erase that cross and in its place I want you to see a flower. I want you to see any flower that you choose, but see it plainly with your eyes closed. *See* it in your mind's eye, and tell me when you have it. "Okay. I see it."

Fine. Now turn that flower into a *rose*. A *red* rose. "It already was a red rose."

Good. Now I am going to give you a series of colors and I want you to see these colors in your mind's eye in the same way you saw the other objects. You don't have to hold these colors in your mind, because that is too difficult. All I want is for you to get a fleeting glimpse of each color as I name it. Ready?

The first color is *Red*. I want you to *see* the color *Red*. Visualize it in any way you choose: a red rose; a red valentine heart; a red drapery at a window; a man wearing a red Santa Claus suit. The color *Red*. I want you to *see* the color *Red*. Tell me when you have it. Take your time. We are in no rush. Don't force it. Just tell me when you have it. "Okay, I see it."

Good. Now the next color I want you to *see* is *Orange*. The color *Orange*. Let it come into your mind's eye. It can be a pile of fresh oranges in the supermarket, a glass of freshly poured orange juice, or a Buddhist monk in his long orange robe. The color *Orange*. Tell me when you *see* it. "Okay."

Good. Now the next color is the color *Yellow*. The color *Yellow*. It can be the yellow of a fresh package of butter; the yellow of an egg yolk on a white plate; the yellow sun in the sky. The color *Yellow*. I want you to *see* *Yellow* in your mind's eye. "Okay."

Excellent. The next color is *Green*. The color *Green*. I want you to *see* the color *Green:* a freshly mown lawn, a tree filled with green leaves, a green plant in a window box. I want you to *see* the color *Green*. "I've got it."

Now the color *Blue*. I want you to *see* the color *Blue*. Bring the color *Blue* into your inner eye: the blue of the ocean, the blue of a clear cloudless sky. The color *Blue*. Take your time. I want the color *Blue*. "Okay."

Now I want you to *see* the color *Violet* or *Lilac*. Maybe an African violet growing in a pot, a lilac bush all in bloom, a lilac dress or scarf. The color *Lilac* or *Violet*. "Right. I've got it."

Good. Now you can open your eyes.

The person opens his eyes, looks at you, and you smile. That wasn't so difficult now, was it? He shakes his head and he smiles. I just wanted to see how good your inner sight was, you say. You did very well indeed. He smiles and makes some comment about the colors and how one was more difficult than the other, but he is pleased with himself and pleased that you have told him he did so well.

(Notice how you have given him the idea that he can *see* things with his eyes closed. This is terribly important. If the person is unable to visualize—to picture—with his mind, then you will not be successful and you might as well stop right here. *Never* attempt to take anyone into a past life who doesn't have the ability to see normal everyday objects and symbols and colors in his imagination. NEVER. Got that?)

Okay, you say to the person, now let's try it for real. Close your eyes, get comfortable, and remember that you're not going to be hypnotized. You are in complete control of your mind and your body at all times. Okay? Now close your eyes. Relax. Let's take the trip.

We are going to go through those colors again, but this time I'd like you to see them as layers in a rainbow. I'd like you to imagine them in thick lines, and as we go *down* from the top layer to the *bottom* layer, I want you to imagine them in a rainbow pattern. Okay?

The top color in the rainbow is *Red*. I want you to see the color *Red*. Remember how you saw it just a few minutes ago? Well, I want you to see it that way again. Tell me when you've got it by lightly raising your right hand. Just lift your right hand slightly when you've seen the color *Red*. The color *Red*. Have you got it? Okay. I'll wait. (The right hand signals.)

Fine. Now the next color *downward* in the rainbow is

*Orange.* I want you to go *down* to the color *Orange. Orange.* Remember how you brought it in the last time? The color *Orange.* Signal when you've got it. (The person signals.)

Good. Now let's go *down* to the color *Yellow. Yellow.* Signal when you have it. (He signals.)

Very good. Now the next layer *down* in the rainbow is *Green.* The color *Green.* Remember how you brought it in before? (He gives the signal without being asked for it.)

Okay. Now *down* to *Blue.* The color *Blue.* (The signal comes again.)

Now to the *last* color . . . the *bottom* layer of the rainbow . . . the *final* color: I want you to visualize the color *Lilac.* (Note: The first time around you have discovered if he has chosen violet or lilac. From now on, use the color he has selected. Don't give him any more choices. For this illustration we'll say that the person has chosen lilac.)

Fine. You are now in the color *Lilac.* This is the final color. You are also at what we call your Alpha Level. This is a state of being in which your Conscious Mind has stepped slightly away from its everyday activity and permits your Sub-Conscious and your Super-Conscious to come in more freely.

I want to remind you that you are in complete control of your mind and body at all times. If you want to stop this at any point all you have to do is open your eyes. Do you understand?

Should there be any unexpected noises like telephones or automobile horns, they won't bother you. They are happening *up here* on my level, not *down there* where you are. Do you understand?

Good. Now I want you to take this lilac color and create a cloud of it around your body. I want you to *see* your body standing there enveloped in a fine misty cloud of the color *Lilac. See* yourself and *see* your body covered with this lilac cloud. Signal with your hand when you *see* this.

This signal comes after a few seconds. *Don't* rush any of this. Let the person take his time. You can afford to wait until he sees himself doing the various things you are asking. Rushing him will only create anxiety that he is not doing it correctly, and he may tell you that he *is* seeing those things just to please you. That you don't need—and neither does he.

Good. Your body is now enveloped in the lilac cloud. In front of you there is a tunnel. It is not a long tunnel, and it is made of white marble. It is a friendly place. There is a white light at the end of this tunnel. Please walk through the tunnel toward the white light. When you get to the white light, tell me. (Here the person may scowl a bit and tell you that he can't see the tunnel, or else that he doesn't want to go in there. Remind him that it is a friendly place and not a long tunnel at all. Tell him that the white light at the end of it is a light of protection and he will feel better when he gets there. It's surprising how many people balk at seeing this tunnel or entering it—yet it is an important part of this exercise.) "Okay," he says, "I'm through the tunnel."

Good. Now at your feet there is a staircase. It is going *downward*. Look *down* at your feet and tell me when you see the steps going *down*. "Okay."

The staircase that is *descending* has twenty-one steps. You are standing at the *top* of the steps. When I start counting the steps I want you to *see* yourself *descending* those steps. I want you to *see* yourself going *down* the steps. Each time I count you will go *down* to the next step. Do you understand? (He nods.)

Okay. You are on the top step. The 21st step. Now let's go *down* to the 20th step.

*Down* to the 19th.

*Down* to the 18th.

*Down* to the 17th.

*Down* to the 16th.

*Down* to the 15th. You are getting deeper and deeper into your Alpha Level.

*Down* to the 14th.

13 . . .

12 . . .

11 . . .

10. Deeper and deeper into your Alpha Level.

9 . . .

8 . . .

7 . . .

6 . . .

5. You are almost to the bottom of the steps.

4 . .

3 . . .

2 . . .

1 .

You are at the bottom of the stairs. You are now at a deeper level of your mind than you have ever been before, yet you are in complete control of your mind and your body at all times. Any time you decide to return up here to my level you only have to open your eyes. Do you understand?

Good.

Look straight ahead of you and you will see a door. Tell me what the door looks like, what it's made of. Is it wood or metal or painted or plain? Tell me what the door looks like. (This door serves three purposes. It gets the person visualizing again, it eventually leads to a whole new landscape in his mind, and it gives you a chance to analyze what kind of a personality he has *after* he has returned from his trip. If the door is heavy, dark, and studded with large nails, then you are dealing with a person who keeps to himself, who doesn't want others prying into his affairs—a lonely and possibly insecure person. The lighter the color of the door and the simpler the decoration on it, the freer that person is with himself, the more open to other people. The boy I spoke about in the section on healing, the one suffering from the malignant brain tumors, had a pure glass door—the first one I've ever encountered. He told me later that he had nothing to hide; he thought his life was over and therefore was open for anyone to examine. Of course you do *not* at this point give your interpretation of the door to the person. That comes afterward, *if you so choose.* You let him describe the door, but you make no comment.)

Now I want you to grasp the door handle and open the door. (He nods, having done it.)

Now you step through the doorway and you find that you are in an open area. There is much sunlight and it is a pleasant place. Do you see this open area? (He nods.)

Now, in front of you, several feet in front of you, there is a wall. Will you walk over to the wall and tell me what it is made of and what color it is? (The wall will give you the same kind of information about the person that the door did. Its most important aspect, however, is that it will act as the focal entryway to this person's past life.)

Okay, now that you have described the wall, I want you to reach out, touch it with your left hand, and start walking down along it, to your right. I want you to walk along the wall and keep walking until you come to *another* door that will be *in* the wall. Keep walking until you come to that doorway and then, when you get there, tell me. (This takes only a few seconds and he nods.) You've found the door? (He nods again or says "Yes.") I want you to open the door and step inside.

You are now in a completely different landscape. Look around and tell me what you see. Trees? What kind of trees? Flowers? What kind of flowers? Buildings? People? Tell me what you see.

This is the point at which the person has stepped into one of his past lives and is about to relive a part of it. As of now, you must be constantly on the alert to lead the person through this particular past life.

From here on, each case history will differ. Because of this, I cannot put down exact guidelines for you to follow. All I can do is tell you of one exceptional case that I handled so you can see how you will have to handle *your* cases.

The man in question lived in Ohio and came to me because he was an artist and wanted to see his past lives from that vantage point. He was positive that he had lived in ancient Greece and in medieval France. He also had some American Indian blood that he was proud of, but that was not of interest to him on this particular day, he told me. I am now going to recreate the entire experience for you. His replies have been put in italics. He has just stepped beyond his wall:

What do you see? *It's someplace outdoors. There are trees and a mountain range off in the distance.*

Have you ever been there before? *I don't know. It sort of looks familiar, but I don't know. It could be anywhere.* Where do you think it is? *I don't know. Anywhere, I guess.* Where do you want to go? To the left? To the right? *There are some trees over there. I'm going to see what's on the other side of them.* (Pause.) What do you see now? *There is nothing there. Just a river and a flat area that leads up into the mountains.* Can you see any people? *No.* Are there any buildings? *No, just the trees and the river and the mountains.* (Pause.) *It seems very strange.* Why? *There should be people here.* What do you mean? *There should be people here. There used to be people here.*

How do you know there used to be people there? *Because I've been here when there were people, and now they've gone.*

Where have they gone? *I don't know, but they aren't here any longer.* Did they live beside the river? Among the trees? *No, they lived in the caves.* What caves? *The caves in those mountains, but they used to farm and graze the animals here, beside the river.* Where do you think they went? *I don't know, but I'm going to go up into the mountains. Maybe someone is in the caves.* Okay. Let me know when you get there. (Long pause.) What's the matter? *The path has overgrown with weeds. It's difficult to walk on it. It never used to be this bad. It was always smooth and clean.* (Pause.) *Okay, I'm at the entrance to one of the caves.* What do you see in there? *Nothing. It's empty.* Where are the people? *I told you they've gone. They've fled.* Fled? *Yes. They were driven away. Now I remember! They came and drove us away. They said they wanted the land! They drove us away and they killed many of us as we were leaving!* Who are "they"? *I don't remember.* Look at your hands. Tell me what color they are. *They're kind of dark.* Like an African native? *No, like an Indian. Like an American Indian's hands.*

Look down at your body. What are you wearing? (Pause.) *Some sort of animal skin thing that hangs around my shoulders and down to my knees. There is a belt around my waist. A very pretty belt.* Can you describe it for me? *Well, it seems to be made out of hammered silver and there are blue stones, turquoise it looks like, set into it.* Where did you get the belt? Did you find it? *No, my people made it. They made it right here. When we lived here in these caves.* Are you a member of the Navajo tribe? *The what?* The Navajo tribe. *I never heard of them.* Never heard of them? *No.* How about the Hopis? Are you a member of that tribe? *I've heard speak about those people, but they live far to the north of here. We never had any contact with them.* Far to the north? *That's what I said.* How far? *Oh, I don't know, maybe seven or ten days' journey away. Maybe more.* But they live in Arizona. *Where?* Arizona. *I don't know where that is.* Well, today they live in Arizona, so if you are ten days' journey to the south, you must be somewhere in northern Mexico. *I don't know.* (Long pause.)

What are you doing? *I'm cleaning out one of the caves.* Why? *Well, I'm going to live here, of course!* (Another long pause.) Now what are you doing? *I went and got some water from the stream. We have a small stream that runs through the village and the water is so pure and sweet. Do you want some?"* (He hands me an invisible water gourd.) No thanks. I don't understand why you have come back to this place. Everyone is gone. You were driven away. Why are you back here? *Because I am an old man and this is my home. I no longer fear them.* Fear who? *The men with the white skins who speak Spanish. I no longer fear them. I've come back to my home and I shall stay here until I die. You see this cave? There are many things that must be done to it. I must put in some rushes for a bed and I must get some wood for a fire. Maybe I can find a dog that is not too wild for companionship. We had lots of dogs in those days. Maybe one or two will smell the smoke and will come to investigate. I'd like to have a dog again. Every man needs*—— (He broke off suddenly and let out a cry.)

What's the matter? *In the entrance to the cave. They are back.* Who's back? *The white men, and they have guns in their hands! They are looking at me and laughing. I think they are going to kill me!*(Another cry.) What happened, did they shoot you? *No, it's my stomach! My stomach is on fire. They are standing there and looking into the cave and watching me and laughing! Oh my God! My stomach is hurting terribly.* (He was almost doubled up on the chair.) *Do you know what they have done? They've poisoned the water in the stream! They poisoned the water and they are letting me die! Oh my God! My stomach!*

(Here I was forced to step in.) Okay. Forget about the pains. You have left your body. You have left your body and you are floating up over it now. All the pains have ceased. (He straightened up in the chair.) Now look down. Can you see your body on the floor of the cave? *Yes.* (There were tears in his eyes.) *I see it.* What do you feel about it? *I'm glad to be rid of it. It was old and weak but it had a proud mind! It went back and died in its ancestral home and I'm proud of it.*

All right, now lift up and out of the cave and return to the grassy area just inside that long wall. Do you remember that place? Where you first came in here? (He nodded.) Okay, go back there. *Okay. I'm back.* Good. Now walk through the doorway. (He nodded.) You are now on the other side of the wall. You are yourself again and in this life. You are (and I used his name) and you are yourself again.

Now walk back down the wall, in the direction you came from. When you get to the first doorway, tell me. (Long pause. *Okay.)* Walk through that door and close it behind you. You are now facing the staircase. Can you see the steps going *up*? (He nodded.) Okay, let's start back up the stairs. See yourself going up the stairs as I count them for you.

You are on the 1st step. Go *up* to the 2nd one.

*Up* to the 3rd.

*Up* to the 4th.

*Up* to the 5th. You are going *upward* now.

*Up* to 6.

*Up* to 7.

*Up* to 8.

*Up* to 9.

*Up* to 10. You are halfway to the top.

11 . . .

12 . . .

13 . . .

14 . . .

15. Almost to the top.

16 . . .

17 . . .

18 . . .

19 . . .

20 . . . ·

21 . . .

You are at the top of the stairs. Now look in front of you. There is that marble corridor. Do you see it? (He nodded.) Okay, start up the corridor. When you get to the end, there will be a *Lilac* light. When you get there you will be covered in a *Lilac* light. Tell me when this happens. *(Okay. I'm in the light.)*

Good. Now the color changes up to *Blue. (Okay.)*

*Up* into Green. (Okay.)

*Up* into *Yellow. (Uh-huh)*

*Up* into *Orange. (Uh-huh).*

And finally, *up into Red! Open your eyes!* You're back up here with me. *Welcome home!*

The person will be a little whoozey for a few moments. Hand him the glass of water and let him sip it (he will probably be very thirsty). While he's doing so, get up from your chair, go into the bathroom and wash your hands, turn on the light—do anything to start some sort of movement around the room that will let him know that the session is over and he's come through it in one piece.

Afterward, you can both discuss what he saw and what he

experienced, playing back the tape, if you wish, and making comments about it.

The person will *always be amazed* that he didn't go back to any place where he *thought* he had lived. If he feels that you have deliberately forced him to go to the particular place and time he did go to, you can always replay the tape to prove that he took *himself* there and that all you did was accompany him and clarify things as he went along.

As I have said, each regression is different, but there are many things you can do to make that particular lifetime come into sharper focus. For instance:

1. To find out what the person's name was in that lifetime, *ask* him. If he doesn't know what he was called, tell him that there is a lovely woman sitting nearby. The woman gets up and walks over to him. She will open her mouth and she will say *one word*—that *one word* will be his first name. Then the woman vanishes.

2. To find out the year, you can always say that there is a calendar on the wall and the *year* is written on the calendar in large black letters. Have him walk over to the wall and read the date on the calendar. Or, you can have him see a newspaper on a table. Have the person walk over to the newspaper and read the date on it. This is also a good method of finding out *where* he was and what language he was speaking.

3. When other people come into the scene, ask him what relationship these people have with him in that particular life. After a few seconds he will tell you that they were his mother and brother, wife, and son, or whatever.

4. Ask him to describe the furnishings of the house if he finds himself in one: the color of the walls, the decoration of the room, and so on. Also have him look out the window. What does he see out there? Windmills? Ice caps? Palm trees? A desert? The sea?

5. Get him to describe what he's wearing. Have him look down at his feet. Are they bare? In sandals? In high boots? In silk slippers? Wooden shoes? What is he wearing on his body? What colors? Materials? What is the fashion?

6. To get a clear picture of his face, have him look in a mirror that is on the wall. Have him describe the face he sees reflected in it. Is it white? Black? Yellow? Old? Young? Smooth? Lined? Bearded?

7. Ask him about his children, his wife . . . his husband. Oh

179

yes! Don't be surprised if a male sitter returns to a female life, or if the woman in front of you discovers that she has been a boy! This is normal rather than unusual in regression trips.

8. Often a sitter will describe personality traits discovered in a past life that will explain certain characteristics in this lifetime. One woman I assisted found herself back in fifteenth-century England as a poor farm girl living in dirt and filth among the animals. "That's why I'm so fussy about my house and my appearance in this life," she told me. "I hated that lifetime and all its dirt!"

Illnesses or other physical markings or defects also can be related to past lives. An arm blown off in an ancient battle aches in this life. A present-life birthmark appears on the site where an old wound was received. Weak eyes now may be reminders of long ago blindness.

I always try to take the person up to the moment of death in each lifetime. Death is always the most memorable fact of each existence, but it must be handled with care. Tell the person he is in the last day of that lifetime. Ask him where he is, who is with him. Is he in bed? At home? In a hospital? How old is he? Does he feel any pain? *Let him talk and tell you.* Then take him up to the last ten minutes of that life. Then the *last minute.* But as soon as he has *died,* tell him to look down and see his body. That way he will be free of all pains and sadness. Ask him how he feels about that body and he will probably tell you that he is glad to be rid of it. Now bring him straight back to the area inside the wall. Have him come through the doorway of the wall over to this side, and then call him by his name in this lifetime. Mention his name several times as he walks back along the wall, through the first door, and starts up the steps.

Each case you handle will be different. Each will require tact and unshakable attention. At no time should you get flustered if the person starts to cry. Simply move him into another stage of that life, saying, "Okay, let's go about ten years into the future. What do you see now?" The tears will usually stop at once. After all, nobody can cry for ten whole years!

# LESSON 19

# A
# Medium-
# istic Circle

Up until World War II it was possible to find an old-fashioned séance in almost every large town in America, and in a lot of small ones as well. Even a tiny place like Newton Falls, Ohio, had its Spiritualist group and weekly séances at the Bailey home, where spirits would talk, trumpets would rise, and objects would appear from out of nowhere. But with the coming of the war and the practicality that period demanded, séances went out of style. There are fashions for everything and a time for everything, and the séance was no longer "in."

Hollywood helped kill it with those Bob Hope or Abbott & Costello flicks in which the medium was almost always a charlatan and the skeletons that appeared over Costello's head were always made of papier-mâché and lowered on a wire by a villain overhead. Then, too, the great Houdini made headlines by traveling around the world debunking every medium he could find. The fact that he believed in spirit guidance and stated in a letter when he was in London that he had attended a séance that was "successful and wonderful" was never made public. Sir Arthur Conan Doyle, the creator of Sherlock Holmes, was a Spiritualist, and his son Adrian was present when Houdini confessed that to admit in public what he really felt about spirit communications would "be a detriment to my work as a magician." Half-truths from celebrities and outright farce on the screen were more responsible than anything else for killing the séance in America.

Of course, there are still a few places where you can go to see a genuine séance, but they are few and far between. The various Spiritualist summer camps like like those in Lilly Dale, Pennsylvania, and Chesterfield, Indiana, claim that their séances are genuine, but the doubters and investigators aren't quite in agreement with them. This is not to say that all the Spiritualist camps are phony, just to point out that quite a bit of their claims have come under great criticism recently from members inside their own ranks.

It's easy to "stage" a fake séance, mostly because everyone wants to believe that what is happening is real. Some people who attend want to be taken in so that they can later brag to their friends that they "spoke" with a spook. Others are aged and lonely, looking for some proof that when they die it won't be the end. They *want* to believe that what they are seeing is the truth.

There are shops around the country where you can buy

trumpets that will float in the dark; "spirit lights," hanging on the end of thin wires, that flicker off and on as if someone from the other world was in the room and using energy; special remote-control radio equipment that sounds as if voices are coming out of the air; and tables with springs hidden in their hollow legs to make them move when the lights are out. It is a good business because gullible people have made it so.

I recall going to a séance in Mexico City in which the medium sat in the center of a darkened room and we, the spectators, sat in a large circle around her. There were no controls on her, she was not tied to her chair, and the room was so pitch-black that you could barely see your hand in front of your face. After a few minutes of mumbled prayers in Spanish from the medium, little lights began to appear; all coming from the center of the room—that is, from near the medium. The lights swooped up into the air and hovered over us. While many of the Mexican ladies (and these were society people, not ignorant peasants) shouted "Oh, thank you, God! Bless you, spirits," the lights traveled and bounced and smoked—yes, *smoked*. One floated very near my face and I could see the thread of smoke coming from it. Another landed on my shirt and I watched it glow and then burn out, to the accompaniment of a barely perceptible odor of chemicals and a mark on my shirt. I had never heard that spirit lights smoked, or that the energy the spirit took to manifest itself would burn clothing. Obviously, the lady had spent some time in an occult shop before the séance began.

Then huge flowers began slapping us in the face. They came from the center of the room, hit our bodies, and sailed past our heads. Again: "Thank you, Jesus! Thank you, spirits!" No one seemed to remember the vase full of yellow chrysanthemums that had been on a table beside the medium's chair before the lights went out. When they came back on again, the bouquet was sadly depleted. The flowers had been flung by the medium. In a genuine séance when flowers appear, there were usually *no flowers* in the room before the session began; they come out of nowhere. This time they came out of a large ceramic vase and their stems were still wet from the water. Yet the majority of people there were most impressed and kept their flowers clutched to their hearts as if God and the spirits had actually blessed these blossoms.

When I was asked my opinion of the séance at the dinner

table afterward, I became rather unpopular. The response was unanimous: *I* was young and inexperienced. *I* didn't know the truth when I saw it. No, but I knew a fake "spirit light" when I saw it and a wet flower when it hit me in the face.

I repeat: People want to believe. They will believe *anything* if they have decided in advance that it is going to be real.

Even mediums can be gullible. Once in Hollywood, when I was president of the California Society for Psychical Research, I asked a magician to give a demonstration on how séances and mediumistic sittings could be faked. It wasn't done to debunk the psychic field, but to show people what they should be wary of and what could be faked to look real.

The magician had a five-year-old boy with him, a cute kid with blond hair and big blue eyes. He asked the little boy to tell him what was in a sealed envelope. The boy did it. Someone came up from the audience and asked the boy a question. The boy answered it correctly. Another person cut a deck of cards and, after removing one from the pack, hid it in a steel box. Could the child identify the card? He did.

I was sitting in the audience beside one of the most respected mediums in Los Angeles, a woman known for her honesty and her devotion to proving the existence of life after death. She was enchanted with the little boy and kept exclaiming "What a wonderful channel that child is! Oh, what great talents in one so young!"

Then the magician explained how he had done each trick. The boy had been coached in trickery for days before the exhibition, knew what signals to look for from the magician, had a transistor listening device tucked under his innocent blond hair—and, in short, was no more clairvoyant than Mrs. Astor's horse. When the tricks had been revealed, the audience was incredulous, yet applauded—everyone except the medium with me. "David, I can't believe that sweet child would stoop so low! Obviously the boy has great mediumistic talents. We can never trust magicians, you know!" She refused to believe that she had been hoaxed even when the hoaxer told her so to her face.

People want to believe.

All through this course, I've given you the basics of the various techniques and then asked you to try them for yourself. You've seen that it is possible to get vibrations from a ring, to

184

contact someone at a distance without picking up the telephone, and even to influence the elements to bring you a material object that you desire. I haven't tried to pull any spirit mumbo-jumbo on you or demand that you *believe*. All I've done is ask you to keep an open mind and then test out what I've said under your own conditions.

That's all I'm asking you to do now in relation to séances. Listen to what I have to say, pay attention to the instructions, and then try it for yourself. Fair enough?

## THE PREPARATION: THE CIRCLE

First of all, don't try a séance until you have prepared yourself. By this I mean don't just sit down at a table on a moment's notice and say, "Okay, spirits, let 'er rip!" It doesn't work that way.

One of the most important elements of any séance is the person who will act as a channel for the information that will be coming through. As in the table-tipping exercise, *your group must have a leader,* someone who has demonstrated his or her psychic abilities, and in whom you have confidence. A séance is not like a baseball game, in which everyone gets a turn at bat. In preparing for a séance, one person is chosen and the entire running of the séance is on that person's shoulders.

Once you have chosen your leader, I would suggest that your group try a few sittings as a "circle." In Great Britain a great deal of emphasis is placed on the circle. The British believe that sitting in a home circle is the best way to develop mediumistic abilities. From that circle will come experiences that will be brought into use later when the actual séance is held.

If you are serious about preparing for a séance, get a group of friends together and agree to meet once a week at the same time and, ideally, in the same place; a private home is usually best. The circle should be composed of those who *really* want their séance to be successful, who believe there is some outside force that can be tapped, and who won't laugh or be sarcastic when the energies start to manifest themselves in the group.

Make sure that the people in the group are *friends*—by that,

I mean compatible. Don't invite Mary if you know she doesn't like Helen; keep Pete out of this if he is jealous of Tom's psychic advancement; and for heaven's sake, keep Margaret's husband away if he doesn't believe in any of this but won't let Margaret go out at night without him.

Your circle will probably take its final form after around the third meeting, as less committed early members drop out, leaving the most seriously committed as the permanent group. This group can be of any size and, if possible, should be divided equally between men and women. That division almost never happens, though; there are always more women than men at such gatherings, mainly because men aren't as willing to publicly exhibit their interest in spirits.

In England it is not unusual for people to sit for five and six years in a circle. I don't ask that much of you, but I do expect you to sit together four to six times before you attempt the séance. (I keep saying *the* séance as if you can only have one of them. Not so. After you've held your first one, then you can keep having them as often as you like. They can come once a week and take the place of your circle.)

The lights should be dimmed or, even better, turned off and only a candle or two left burning nearby.

You should have prerecorded a cassette tape. It should be done on a sixty-minute side so that it can be left on after the spoken and musical part has finished, with no one having to worry about getting up to turn it off. This tape should start out with a prayer—not a long oration, but a simple request for strength, protection, and guidance. I won't tell you what to say. It should be the work of your group; that way it will belong to you and not to me, and it will say what *your* group wants it to say.

Following this prayer you should have a five- to ten-minute relaxation exercise on the tape. Possibly you'll want to use the color countdown, going down the steps and into your Secret Places. Once there, you'll all relax and try to still your Conscious Minds as much as possible. The voice on the tape should be soft and soothing, and should create the idea that mental relaxation is a highly desired condition. It should also inspire confidence that no matter what happens, everyone in the group is protected. Once again, write this mood-inducing exercise to suit yourselves. After that there should be a long session of soft music without horns, base drums, and loud cymbals. The group I led in Los Angeles used harp music, and it was quite appropriate.

All the members of the group have their eyes closed and are sitting comfortably. It is *not* necessary to have your legs and arms uncrossed and your palms upward on your lap, but by doing so you will have the feeling that you are "open" and ready to "receive" whatever it is that wishes to come in.

You have seen, when we did psychometry and some of the other exercises (especially bringing in the colors for the first time), that it isn't easy to "make your mind a blank," even though all books on psychic techniques insist on it. You can never make your mind a complete blank, so don't try. What you *can* do is relax your mind to a point at which you don't have quite so many unconnected ideas dashing in and out.

This can be done by thinking of one object (usually a flower or a cross or a scene from nature that you like very much) and bringing that image back into your mind each time another thought comes along and knocks it out of the way. Making your mind "a blank" takes concentration—just the opposite of what the words seem to imply you're doing.

*The leader of the group will not have her eyes closed.* She must remain alert, watching the faces around her at all times. Ideally, she will have been involved in this sort of activity long enough that she no longer feels the need for basic "instruction." If you can possibly persuade a professional medium in your area to help you in the first few circle meetings, all the better. Even if you have to pay her, it's worth it.

As you sit quietly, all sorts of things will come to your mind. You may take a trip, soaring over mountains and through treetops. You may go back a few years in time and be a child in your family home. You may see the faces of people you've not thought of in years. You may hear voices and see symbols you cannot explain. Try to remember as much of this as you can because when the leader of the circle asks you to open your eyes, he or she will go from person to person and you will be expected to relate what you experienced.

As you tell what you "saw," others in the group may try to interpret your images. That can be both good and bad. The images belong to you—they were given to you—and therefore the only one who can really understand their meaning is you yourself. You received these impressions from a Super-Conscious level. The others are offering their interpretations on a Conscious level. Listen to what they have to say, if you choose to, but let the final interpretation be your own. Got that?

There may come a time during the silence when you have the urge to talk aloud. In the beginning, fight this urge. It may not be anything more than a desire to break the quiet of the room or, even worse, to give your Conscious ego center stage. If the "message" that you are being urged to say comes back again and again, and won't go away no matter how you change your thought pattern, then open your mouth and say whatever it is. Tell what you see and tell how you are feeling *inside* as this information is pressed upon you. Do not try to interpret what you are seeing or what you have said— that's not your job. If the message was really from "spirit," it should have been given with enough clarity that you need provide no further explanation.

In the beginning you may feel shy or backward about speaking up when everyone else is silent. Fine. Never open your mouth to vocalize anything unless the urge to do so is so great you can't withstand it. I can't define the phenomenon any better than that—you'll see for yourself what sensations are involved when you begin to practice this.

The reason for this silence and waiting is for you all to clear yourselves so that "spirit" can use you as a channel—a radio channel or a television channel, if you can imagine it. As I've insisted all through this book, *you* are an instrument that is to be used when the condition of the instrument and the conditions around the instrument are in working harmony.

Let's destroy a few myths:

1) There is no need for you to be taken over so completely by "spirit" that you don't know what you are doing or saying. In almost every case of trance mediumship, the instrument knows what is happening, even though he is not controlling it. For instance, he knows that words are forming in his mind and are coming out of his mouth, despite the fact that he may not be able to repeat them later.

2) If someone starts to give a message, pay attention to the flow of the sentences. While content is important, in the beginning the *ease* (or lack of) in which a message is given is very

significant. If the message is given evenly and with very few pauses, it is more likely a product of spirit than of the sitter's own mind. One of the best ways to test this afterward is to have the sitter *consciously* give the group a few minutes' talk on the same subject. If she was being used as an instrument, her *conscious* message will be halting, full of "ah's," and "you know," and so forth.

3) There is no need to go into gymnastics when the message is being delivered. The spirit is using only your vocal chords and the muscles of your mouth. Beware of people who insist on jumping up and acting out the part of a Chinese or an American Indian, or rapturously (and long-windedly) admire invisible beads on an invisible robe. Save the theatrics for your little-theater group.

4) Don't let anyone tell you who your guide is—not in the beginning, anyway. Find out for yourself. I've known so many people who were told by well-meaning friends or a well-meaning leader that their guide was a "tall black African" or "a Hindu with a white turban," and this influenced the manner in which they gave their messages. If they *consciously* believed that their guide was Chinese, then they would twist up their eyes, hunch in their shoulders, and put their hands together in what they assumed was a humble Oriental attitude. Your guide needs no outward physical manifestations. If, after a while, you find your body doing those things naturally, fight it. If the behavior persists (especially after you are "out of it"), then don't fight. You'll see what I mean as time goes on.

5) Still in the same vein: There is no need to speak in accents. The "spirit," or guide, is not speaking directly; he is mentally using your vocal chords and you are mentally translating what he says before you let the words out of your mouth. Granted, all this happens quite quickly and you will not be aware of the process. But there is still no reason why you should speak with a Chinese accent or use words like "wigwam" for house and "moon" for month. Old-timers will disagree with me, but I don't care. I have one of the best authorities in Spiritualism on my side in this matter: the late, great Englishman, Harry Edwards. They can argue with his spirit the next time it appears at a séance!

6) There are some who claim that your shoes should be off so that you have contact with the floor. Others claim you

shouldn't wear rubber-soled shoes. If the energy comes from above and into your head, I don't know what the feet have to do with it. Rubber soles are good if you are an electrician and working near water, but they have nothing to do with "spirit" energies. If you feel more comfortable with your shoes off, by all means remove them—but don't do it thinking it's going to help your mediumship!

7) The reason for establishing a regular weekly meeting time for the circle is to keep you from being bombarded for the other six days by a guide that wants to come through. Once you get started on this, you may attract an entity that enjoys the contact as much as you do; but you can't allow him to take over whenever he wishes. If you are in the supermarket or having dinner in a restaurant, it would be damned embarrassing to find yourself suddenly stopping dead still, closing your eyes, and making obscure references to the world of spirit. If you feel the sensation coming on (and you'll be able to "feel it" once you've experienced it), give the intruding spirit a firm but definite No. Tell him to wait for the next meeting of the circle. If he is any friend at all, he'll wait. If not, get rid of him simply by telling him to go away each time he starts to bother you. Spirits, like people, can take a hint. They know when they're not wanted.

# LESSON 20

# An Old-Fashioned Séance

You may want to keep on with your circle meetings indefinitely. Possibly so much will be coming from them that you won't want to try the physical manifestations of a séance. Maybe by that time you'll feel that a séance is beneath you, that you have become more spiritual and no longer need the outward signs that spirit and guides are around you.

Fine. That's what I would like to see happen, but if it doesn't, or if you are just plain curious about what a séance is like, then here's what to do:

Choose a date when most of the people in the circle will be free to attend, and find a suitable place—preferably the same home where the circle has been taking place, since most of you will feel comfortable there by this time. However, if you haven't been holding the circle meetings, then any place that is relatively quiet will do—but don't expect perfect results if you haven't been holding regular circles.

The room must have a rather large table, big enough to seat the members of the séance all around it. It's best to have each person sitting down, rather than have a few standing. If there is a large group (and I do not recommend this for the first few times), then you can have some people seated at the table and the others seated, auditorium-style, watching from a distance.

Do not put a cloth on the table. Leave it bare.

In the center of the table:

a. Spread a deck of cards.
b. Put a bowl of water with several cut flowers floating in it.
c. Have an incense burner with rosewood or sandalwood incense ready to light.
d. Have a pad and ball-point pen near the center.
e. Prepare a cassette tape with soft music ready to turn on.
f. Have two white candles ready to burn. These should not be on the table itself but be placed at some distance from it, so that the room is slightly illuminated.
g. Make sure that all telephones are silenced and that a note has been put on the door to the house saying that you are not to be disturbed for any reason.
h. Pull the draperies across the windows to keep all light out from other sources and also to help muffle outside noises.

Choose a leader, a medium, who will be in complete command. This should be someone whom you all trust and who has had experience in psychic phenomena. Possibly your own circle has turned up one person who receives the spirits easier than the others. This is the person who should lead the activities.

All sit around the table. The leader lights the candles, lights the incense, puts on the music, turns off the lights, and seats herself in the *center chair.*

Everyone joins hands and the leader offers up a prayer asking for strength, protection, and guidance—especially protection and guidance. It would be wise if the medium thinks about this prayer for a while to deliver exactly what she wants to say rather than make it up as she goes along, confusing herself and others with random thoughts.

After the prayer, hands are released and placed *palms down* on the table.

Then the waiting begins.

The leader will ask that a spirit come into the room, that an entity will manifest itself for the group. She should use phrases like "We are ready" and "We are open to receive you." She should repeat this again and again, and everyone should be on the alert for the tiniest off-stage noise or movement. Those around the table can also ask, from time to time, that a spirit come in and manifest itself, but the main responsibility for this "summoning of the spirits" rests on the shoulders of the medium.

From here on, there is no set formula or pattern. You will have to cope with situations as they arise. Be prepared to react, to observe, to experience. Don't get panicky. If you are frightened, you shouldn't be there in the first place.

Here are some of the things to look for:

1. The medium (the leader) may suddenly go into trance. She may shudder or even cry out, and her head will droop. Don't let anybody say anything or make any movement. For God's sake, *don't touch her,* because as in the astral projection exercise she may no longer be in her own body! She will be gone and an entity may be inside her instead. Soon she will lift her head and begin to speak. It may be a message for someone sitting at the table, or it may be a general address for mankind. You'll find that spirits love to pontificate. If your name is called and you are asked questions by the trance voice, respond. Don't sit there like a stick of wood. Speak to the voice  Answer its questions and ask some of your own. Answer in a reasonable

tone of voice; don't whisper or mumble. When that entity leaves, the medium may come back to her Conscious self, or she may stay "under" and a new entity will come through using her vocal chords and body. When she is finished—or rather when "they" are finished with her—she will straighten up, probably sigh deeply, and shake her head to clear away some of the cobwebs. If the session has been taped, all the better. Possibly the medium won't recall half the things she said, because it *wasn't* she who was doing the talking.

2. Perhaps *you* or someone in the circle will be taken into trance, or start delivering a speech, or begin to twitch and shudder. Maybe you will drop your head on the table, unable to lift it. Maybe the woman next to you will begin to talk gibberish, and shake her head so that her hairdo comes undone. Maybe the boy at the end of the table will be urged to reach out, grab the pen and paper, and start writing. If these events begin happening, *the leader of the session should take charge* and guide the entity who has come in. The leader should ask the entity questions and should converse with it. The leader should try and chase away the spirit that is talking foolishness and get the girl with the flying hair to calm down. The leader must be in command at all times and the entities must obey her. If they do not want to, then the leader should call a halt to the entire proceedings and have the lights turned on at once. Under no circumstances should matters be allowed to get out of control.

3. Perhaps some force will move the cards that have been fanned out in the center of the table. One card might be pulled out from the rest, or even tossed onto the floor. There may be some "mystical" reason that certain cards are chosen while the others remain undisturbed, but the cards are really there to give the spirit-energy one more way to manifest itself.

4. Perhaps the spirits will decide to pick up a few flowers and toss them around the table. Maybe they will deliver one of the flowers to someone at the table. If you get one, don't scream and pass out. Say "Thank you." You've been honored.

5. Perhaps other flowers or objects will suddenly appear in the room from elsewhere. I attended a session once at which vases of daisies stood on the table, yet red roses were delivered to everyone. Another time, a man felt a weight on his lap. A

heavy book had been placed there—a book that hadn't even been in the house, let alone in that room.

Once, at a séance in the class in Hollywood, things were going slowly when suddenly one girl's hand was raised about six inches from the table. She complained that she couldn't put it back down. As we all stared, the faintest impression of a kitten appeared between her hand and the tabletop. She said that she could feel the fur and the warmth, and most of us said "A kitten" in unison. Then it vanished and her hand was lowered to the table once more.

There are no set rules and regulations for what will happen once a séance has begun. You have to be willing to accept anything and everything as it is handed (or thrown!) to you.

Above all, don't be frightened. There is nothing to be afraid of. I don't know of anyone who was ever killed by a ghost . . . scared silly, but *never* killed!


That's it. You've come to the end of the book and the end of the course. By now you have done things you thought you'd never be doing, and seen things happen that you'd thought impossible.

I cannot go any farther with you.

I've opened the door.

You must continue on your own.

Good luck and God bless.

Oh yes: Don't forget to *listen!*

# INDEX

# INDEX